JOHN BUNYAN

FACSIMILE OF A LETTER WRITTEN BY JOHN BUNYAN TAKEN FROM "THE CHURCH BOOK OF BUNYAN MEETING."

By permission of the Trustees of Bunyan Meeting, Bedford.

JOHN BUNYAN

A STUDY IN PERSONALITY

BY

G. B. HARRISON, M.A.

ARCHON BOOKS
1967

FIRST PUBLISHED 1928
J. M. Dent & Sons Limited

REPRINTED 1967 IN AN UNALTERED
AND UNABRIDGED EDITION

LIBRARY OF CONGRESS CATALOG CARD NUMBER: 67-14501
PRINTED IN THE UNITED STATES OF AMERICA

PREFACE

IN this short study, I have tried to trace the development of the mind and the personality of John Bunyan as shown in his writings. The book is not concerned with the value of his " message," but I hope that, by viewing his life and writings in a somewhat new perspective, something will be added to the knowledge of Bunyan's achievement.

The most important sources for Bunyan's biography are his own *Grace Abounding*, with its sequels ; the manuscript *Church Book of Bunyan Meeting* ; the brief life added to the 1700 edition of *Grace Abounding* ; Charles Doe's remarks, principally in the preface to the 1692 folio edition of Bunyan's works. Of more modern works, students owe most to the late Dr. John Brown's *John Bunyan : his Life, Times, and Work* (Tercentenary Edition, 1928, edited with valuable additions by F. Mott Harrison). Page references are to G. Offor's edition of *The Works of John Bunyan*.

G. B. H.

CONTENTS

CHAPTER I

THE CONVERT

CHAPTER I

IN the fifty years that followed the death of James the First the history of England was mostly made by the Puritans; but they contributed little of permanent value to its literature. Two names stand out, John Milton and John Bunyan; and even Milton can scarcely be called a true Puritan, for to him the Bible was but one of many books. Bunyan remains, in his writings and in his life, as the essence and epitome of English Puritanism.

Puritanism is an unattractive creed, and its holiness is not beautiful; for its power comes from a rigorous denial of all that appeals to the senses. It demands an intense self-discipline for an end which to the sceptic seems too uncertain to be worth the effort, and to the Catholic to savour of a churlish refusal to use God's good gifts. But such self-discipline in religion has its material compensations, for it over-flows into business, and the Puritan often gathers up in this world what the prodigal has scattered. Moreover, his rigid self-sufficiency is the best of qualities for the pioneer and empire-builder.

The spirit of Puritanism existed among the English people long before the Reformation, but the name denotes a particular creed. This creed is based on the Bible, and nothing but the Bible; its doctrines can only be held by those who regard the Bible as the direct voice of a jealous and stern God. The Puritan opened his Bible at the first chapter of Genesis, and his whole conception of the relationship between God and man depended on belief in an actual covenant made first between God and the man Adam, and, later in the wilderness, between Moses, as God's factor, and the Israelites. Hence the New Testament was but a fulfilling of the Old, and, though it substituted Grace for the old condemnation of the Law, Christ was but an instrument of God's will, whose sayings were of no greater importance than God's words, spoken with his own mouth, at the giving of the Old Covenant.

All faiths are liable to decompose into superstition, and the worship of a book is not less dangerous than the veneration of an image or a ceremony ; whilst excessive adoration of a symbol softens the intellect, idolatry of a text hardens the heart. Yet Puritans were not alone in their attitude towards the Bible. Most Englishmen in the seventeenth century regarded it as the last Court of Appeal, though with Anglican divines the Bible was one of many books ; and Hooker, at the end of his first book *Of the Laws of Ecclesiastical Polity*, answered the Puritan claim to base all law and conduct on the Scriptures alone : " For as they rightly maintain that God must be glorified in all things, and that the actions of men cannot tend unto his glory unless they be framed

12

after his law ; so it is their error to think that the only law which God hath appointed unto men in that behalf is the sacred Scripture."

But, with all doctors of religion, the arguments of an opponent serve chiefly to strengthen their own convictions. The Puritans, especially when their faith was tested by the trials of the Civil War and later in the persecution under the Restoration, more and more withdrew within the covers of their Bibles, refusing to take any notice of intellectual movements in the world outside, where the rigid conception of the scientific truth of the Scriptures was beginning to break down.

With the change of attitude towards the Old Testament the Puritan dogma has crumbled. If there was no first Adam, there was no actual compact between him and God ; the sacrifice on Calvary ceases to be the bloody retribution for Adam's sin, and a new interpretation must be sought if the Bible is still to be regarded as a record of God's dealings with man.

It is difficult for an educated man in the twentieth century, accustomed to see the natural laws of God revealed through the microscope, to realise the full horror of literal belief in the Old Testament ; but it is illustrated very clearly in the development of the mind of John Bunyan.

The records of Bunyan's family and early life are meagre, but they dispose of the legend that Bunyan was a wandering tinker. The family had been long settled in Elstow near Bedford, and there are several entries relating to them in the parish registers and other public records. His grandfather, Thomas Bunyan (who died in 1641), is described in his will as a petty chapman, and owned his own cottage. His father, Thomas Bunyan, junior, was baptized on 24th February 1603 ; on the 10th January 1623 he married Anne Pinney. She died in 1627, and on the 23rd of May the widower married Margaret Bentley. Thomas Bunyan, junior, is described in his will as a brazier. John Bunyan, their son, was baptized on 30th November 1628.

These details can be supplemented from *Grace Abounding*, the record of his spiritual experiences which Bunyan wrote in 1666. *Grace Abounding*, however, is not entirely satisfactory as an historical document, for Bunyan was less concerned with external and material things than with " the manner of his conversion, his sight and trouble for sin, his dreadful temptations, also how he despaired of God's mercy, and how the Lord at length through Christ did deliver him from all the guilt and terror that lay upon him."

The biographer in short must interpret *Grace Abounding* in his own terms, gleaning such facts as are given and arranging them in a new perspective, when perhaps they will take on a new significance.

THE CONVERT

Of his childhood Bunyan says little ; of his parents
even less. They were of " that rank that is meanest
and most despised of all the families in the land."
But they were not paupers. " When we remember
that the wills of his father and grandfather, and of
his maternal grandmother, have been preserved
in the Registry of the District Court of Probate
from a time when the poorest of the poor never made
any wills at all, and that the house in which he was
born had been the property of his ancestors from
time immemorial, it would seem as if Bunyan, in his
humility, had depreciated the social position of his
family more than he had need." [1]

Bunyan was sent to school to learn both to read
and to write ; " the which also I attained, according
to the rate of other poor men's children ; though
to my shame I confess, I did soon lose that little I
learned, and that even almost utterly and long before
the Lord did work his gracious work of conversion
upon my soul." There is exaggeration here. Bunyan did not forget how to read ; he had read not
a little in his youth, not always in works of edification, and in *Grace Abounding* he frequently mentions
his reading. Nor did he forget to write ; for his
writing, of which specimens survive in the *Church
Book of Bunyan Meeting*, though not cultured, is
fluent, with none of the crawling rotundity of one

[1] J. Brown, *John Bunyan, his Life, Times, and Work*, 1928,
p. 29.

who learns to write late in life ; nor indeed could anyone whose pen moved heavily have written with the blistering heat of invective that scorches the pages of some of his earlier works.

He says little of his life at home or in his boyhood, but that little is important. As a child he was much afflicted with fearful dreams and visions—

For often after I had spent this and the other day in sin, I have in my bed been greatly afflicted while asleep with the apprehensions of devils and wicked spirits, who still, as I then thought, laboured to draw me away with them, of which I could never be rid.

Also I should, at these years, be greatly afflicted and troubled with the thoughts of the fearful torments of Hell-fire ; still fearing that it would be my lot to be found, at last, among those devils, and hellish fiends, who are there bound down with the chains and bonds of darkness, unto the judgment of the great Day.

These things, I say, when I was but a child, about nine or ten years old, did so distress my soul, that then, in the midst of my many sports, and childish vanities, amidst my vain companions, I was often much cast down and afflicted in my mind therewith ; yet could I not let go my sins. Yea, I was also then so overcome with despair of life and Heaven, that I should often wish, either that there had been no Hell, or that I had been a devil ; supposing they were only tormentors, that if it must needs be, that I indeed

16

went thither, I might be rather a tormentor, than be tormented myself.

From these words there stands out a clear picture of Bunyan at the age of ten, a highly sensitive, over-strung little boy who wilted visibly before the lurid suggestions of what awaited the sinner in another world ; and since successful methods of punishment are liable to be repeated, it is not unlikely that Bunyan was often reminded of the worm that dieth not. If so, his parents were ultimately the cause of the awful mental sufferings of his early manhood. The success of this mode of appeal to the imagination depended on the fact that he was abnormally fascinated by words and verbal rhythms, both those which he heard and those which he created for himself, though the first manifestations of self-expression took the form of " cursing, lying and blaspheming the holy name of God," in which, as he notes, he had but few equals. After a while these dreams were thrust under, and he developed into a young man of strong passions, with a dominant personality, " the very ringleader of all the youth that kept me company." He played games, danced, rang the church bells, and lived a normal life with the rest of the youths of Elstow. On the whole he had few startling adventures. Once he fell into a creek of the sea, and hardly escaped drowning ; another time he fell out of a boat into Bedford river.

B

In 1644, being now of military age, he was imprested for service with the Commonwealth army, and his name has been found in muster-rolls of the troops serving at Newport Pagnell on 30th November, 1644.[1] In April 1647 he volunteered with the rest of his company for service in Ireland, but though sent as far as Chester he seems not to have crossed the seas ; in July he was disbanded. The only indication in *Grace Abounding*—and that added as an afterthought in the Second Edition—that two and a half years of his adolescence were spent in the army is in this short paragraph :

This also have I taken notice of with thanksgiving ; when I was a soldier, I, with others, were drawn out to go to such a place to besiege it ; but when I was just ready to go, one of the company desired to go in my room ; to which, when I had consented, he took my place ; and coming to the siege, as he stood sentinel, he was shot into the head with a musket bullet, and died.[2]

Bunyan did not care to be too particular about the details of his unregenerate days. Later in life he shuddered at the enormities of his youth.

Yea, such prevalency had the lusts and fruits of the flesh in this poor soul of mine, that had not a miracle of precious Grace prevented, I had not only

[1] Brown, p. 46 ; Editor's Addenda.
[2] *Grace Abounding*, § 13.

perished by the stroke of Eternal Justice, but had also laid my self open, even to the stroke of those Laws, which bring some to disgrace, and open shame, before the face of the world.[1]

From these words it is not clear whether his sins were acted or desired; with his conversion he drew a line under the old account, and turned over to a new leaf. Years afterwards when accused " that I had my misses, my whores, my bastards, yea two wives at once," he denied it indignantly : " I know not whether there be such a thing as woman breathing under the orbs of the whole Heaven, but by their apparel, their children, or by common fame, except my wife. And in this I admire the wisdom of God, that he made me shy of women from my first conversion until now." Nor is he more definite about the rest of his lapses, but then Bunyan's catalogue of sins was comprehensive.

At the same time, his conscience was still sensitive.

But this I well remember ; that though I could myself sin with the greatest delight and ease, and also take pleasure in the vileness of my companions ; yet even then, if I have at any time seen wicked things by those who professed goodness, it would make my spirit tremble. As once, above all the rest, when I was in my highth of vanity, yet hearing one to swear, that was reckoned for a religious man, it had

[1] *Grace Abounding*, § 9.

so great a stroke upon my spirit, that it made my heart to ache.[1]

On the whole though, he was descending the nine steps of Apostasy, which, as Christian told Hopeful, Sinners go down to their destruction :

1. They draw off their thoughts all that they may from the remembrance of God, death and judgment to come.

2. Then they cast off by degrees private duties, as closet-prayer, curbing their lusts, watching, sorrow for sin, and the like.

3. Then they shun the company of lively and warm Christians.

4. After that they grow cold to public duty, as hearing, reading, godly conference, and the like.

5. Then they begin to pick holes, as we say, in the coats of the godly, and that devilishly, that they may have a seeming colour to throw religion (for the sake of some infirmity they have spied in them) behind their backs.

6. Then they begin to adhere to, and associate themselves with, carnal, loose and wanton men.

7. Then they give way to carnal and wanton discourse in secret ; and glad are they if they can see such things in any that are counted honest, that they may the more boldly do it through their example.

8. After this they begin to play with little sins openly.

9. And then being hardened, they show themselves as they are. Thus being launched again into the

---

[1] *Grace Abounding,* § 11.

gulf of misery, unless a special miracle of grace prevent it, they everlastingly perish in their own deceivings.

And then Bunyan married.

There is no record of his marriage, and the name of his wife is unknown; but of the two she would seem to have had the stronger personality, for Bunyan, though always a leader, was as yet not sure where he wanted to go; his wife had already found a pattern of conduct in her dead father. Henceforward Bunyan's daily conduct was observed and measured by the recording angel at home, and to his intense humiliation he found that the standards admired in the village of Elstow seemed tawdry and contemptible in the eyes of his wife. It was not so much that she criticised him directly, but she would often be telling him what a godly man her father was, and how he would reprove and correct vice, both in his house and amongst his neighbours; what a strict and holy life he lived in his days, both in word and deed. Moreover, she had brought as her contribution to the household two books, *The Plain Man's Pathway to Heaven* and *The Practice of Piety*, which her father had left her when he died. These they read together; as yet they failed to bring any conviction to Bunyan, but they remained in the house.

Bunyan's mind being now turned towards religion,

he began to go to church regularly, and for a time passed through the phase of religious mysticism which often manifests itself in early manhood. He adored " high place, priest, clerk, vestments, service and what else belonged to the Church." He became, in short, the devout Anglo-Catholic, finding his spiritual longings satisfied in the ceremonial of the Church, whilst outside he enjoyed much the same life as before.

It is not a little surprising to find the full church ritual persisting in Elstow in 1650, for the liturgy had been abolished by Act of Parliament in 1645.[1] Still, the rector of Elstow, the Rev. Christopher Hall, who had been instituted in 1639 when Laud was Archbishop, was undisturbed throughout the Commonwealth and remained after the Restoration; a fact which suggests that he was a man of considerable piety, and well liked by his parishioners. At any rate, he had a strong influence over Bunyan at this time, for shortly afterwards he preached a sermon on keeping the Sabbath Day, and the evil of breaking it with labour, sports, or otherwise. This greatly touched Bunyan's conscience, as it seemed that he was specially aimed at, and for a little time he was much distressed; but only until dinner-

[1] Brown, pp. 55-6. Sabbath games were abolished in 1644. Another possible explanation is that Bunyan has postdated these experiences by at least five years; but this seems unlikely. If it were so, it would discredit the truth of the narrative.

time. After dinner he went out to play tip-cat. When his turn came to bat, he struck the first blow and was about to strike the second, when a sentence suddenly echoed through his brain, " Wilt thou leave thy sins and go to heaven ; or have thy sins and go to hell ? "

At this [he records] I was put to an exceeding maze ; wherefore, leaving my cat upon the ground, I looked up to Heaven and was as if I had, with the eyes of my understanding, seen the Lord Jesus looking down upon me, as being very hotly displeased with me, and as if he did severely threaten me with some grievous punishment for these, and other my ungodly practices.

I had no sooner thus conceived in my mind, but suddenly this conclusion was fastened on my spirit (for the former hint did set my sins again before my face), that I had been a great and grievous sinner, and that it was now too late for me to look after Heaven ; for Christ would not forgive me, nor pardon my transgressions. Then I fell to musing upon this also ; and while I was thinking of it and fearing lest it should be so, I felt my heart sink in despair, concluding it was too late ; and therefore I resolved in my mind, I would go on in sin. For, thought I, if the case be thus, my state is surely miserable ; miserable if I leave my sins, and but miserable if I follow them ; I can but be damned ; and if it must be so, I had as good be damned for many sins, as be damned for few.[1]

[1] *Grace Abounding*, §§ 22, 23.

This thought bred in him a kind of desperation;
if he was not to go to heaven at least he would
enjoy all the sins he could while on earth.

About a month afterwards, as he was standing
before a neighbour's shop window, cursing and
swearing in his usual way, the woman of the house,
who was herself a " very loose and ungodly wretch,"
rebuked him roundly, as the ungodliest fellow for
swearing that she ever heard in all her life; and
that he was able to spoil all the youth in the whole
town, if they came but in his company. This check,
coming from such a quarter, was most humiliating;
and Bunyan thereupon resolved to quit swearing.

He now began to read his Bible, especially the
historical part; the Epistles of Paul he could not
abide. Outwardly at least he became a reformed
character; to the great admiration of the neighbours,
who commented very favourably on so notable a
conversion. This outward reformation, however,
was not without its struggles. Bell-ringing had been
one of his favourite amusements—

But my conscience beginning to be tender, I thought
such practice was but vain, and therefore forced
myself to leave it, yet my mind hankered; wherefore I should go to the steeple-house, and look on,
though I durst not ring: But I thought this
did not become religion neither, yet I forced myself,
and would look on still: But quickly after, I began
to think, How if one of the bells should fall? Then

24

THE CONVERT

I chose to stand under a main beam, that lay over-
thwart the steeple, from side to side, thinking there
I might stand sure. But then I should think again,
Should the bell fall with a swing, it might first hit
the wall, and then rebounding upon me, might kill
me, for all this beam. This made me stand in the
steeple-door; and now, thought I, I am safe enough;
for if a bell should then fall, I can slip out behind
these thick walls, and so be preserved notwith
standing.

So after this, I would yet go to see them ring,
but would not go further than the steeple-door;
but then it came into my head, How if the steeple
itself should fall? And this thought—it may fall
for ought I know—when I stood and looked on,
did continually so shake my mind, that I durst not
stand at the steeple-door any longer, but was forced
to flee, for fear the steeple should fall upon my head.

Another thing was my dancing; I was a full
year, before I could quite leave that; but all this
while, when I thought I kept this or that Commandment, or did, by word or deed, anything that I thought
were good, I had great peace in my conscience;
and should think with myself, God cannot choose
but be now pleased with me; yea, to relate it in
my own way, I thought no man in England could
please God better than I.[1]

This year must have been a time of constant
emotional strain. In any community it is difficult
enough for a man to leave the company of the wicked

[1] *Grace Abounding*, §§ 33–5.

and join himself to the godly without some comment from the deserted party, much less in the village herd. If the righteous praised the new convert, the ungodly mocked and said bitter things. But mockery at least gives the victim satisfaction that he is following great examples, and suffering as all the saints had suffered. At the worst the village reprobate could hurt the body and sear the mind of the convert with his jibes. The village atheist was a more dangerous enemy, because more subtle ; besides, the arguments are not all on one side, and when the enemy got in with a shrewd blow Bunyan was still too uncertain of himself and of the foundations of his belief to be quite sure where the truth lay. Many of the temptations and terrible sayings which so tormented Bunyan sprouted from certain doubts and phrases sown in his mind in religious argument ; for by this time he was a very brisk talker in matters of religion.

It is not surprising that in the conflicts of this year the mental torments of his childhood returned in an aggravated and maturer form. It was no longer simply material conceptions of devils and hell-fire, but those subtle and tormenting intellectual questions which have puzzled philosophers since men first learned to divide their speech into words. There are problems which must be faced by an honest thinker ; the sceptic is usually left with an optimistic or melancholy agnosticism ; the religious mind will find an emotional or intuitive solution where reason fails to provide an answer satisfactory to the intellect. Bunyan was in the pitiable state of regarding these ultimate problems as peculiar to himself and intimately linked with his own eternal salvation.

The real conflict in his mind was between the three most potent forces which make up the human personality: physical desire, reason, and intuition. His intuitions had been warped and distorted in childhood, his reason and his flesh rebelled; but in the end intuition prevailed over the other two and forced them into his service, or rather reason and body were too weary to continue the struggle any longer. Moreover, words began to have more power than ever over his mind. His brain would catch up a text, and tom-tom its rhythms with an interminable, monotonous iteration until Bunyan was wrought into a state of bodily hysteria. Added to this was his instinctive habit of dramatising his intellectual experiences and expressing them in the form of symbol and allegory.

One of the first stages in his conversion was when he happened upon some three or four poor women in Bedford, sitting at a door in the sun talking about the things of God.

Their talk was about a new birth, the work of God on their hearts, also how they were convinced of their miserable state by nature; they talked how God had visited their souls with his love in the Lord Jesus, and with what words and promises they had been refreshed, comforted and supported against the temptations of the Devil. Moreover, they reasoned of the suggestions and temptations of Satan in particular; and told to each other, by which they had been afflicted, and how they were borne up under his assaults. They also discoursed of their own wretchedness of heart, of their unbelief; and did contemn, slight and abhor their own righteousness, as filthy and insufficient to do them any good.

And methought they spake, as if joy did make them speak; they spake with such pleasantness of Scripture-language, and with such appearance of Grace in all they said, that they were to me, as if they had found a new world, as if they were " people that dwelt alone, and were not to be reckoned amongst their neighbours " (Num. xxiii. 9).[1]

This experience, recollected in tranquillity, returned thus :

About this time, the state and happiness of these poor people at Bedford was thus, in a dream or vision, presented to me. I saw, as if they were set on the sunny side of some high mountain, there refreshing themselves with the pleasant beams of the sun, while I was shivering and shrinking in the cold, afflicted with frost, snow and dark clouds. Methought also, betwixt me and them, I saw a wall that did compass about this mountain; now through

[1] *Grace Abounding,* §§ 37, 38.

this wall my soul did greatly desire to pass ; concluding, that if I could, I would go even into the
very midst of them and there also comfort myself
with the heat of their sun.

About this wall I thought myself to go again and
again, still prying as I went, to see if I could find
some way or passage, by which I might enter therein ;
but none could I find for some time. At the last,
I saw, as it were, a narrow gap, like a little doorway,
in the wall, through which I attempted to pass ; but
the passage being very strait and narrow, I made
many efforts to get in, but all in vain, even until I
was well nigh quite beat out by striving to get in ;
at last with great striving, methought I at first did
get in my head, and after that, by a sideling striving,
my shoulders, and my whole body. Then was I
exceeding glad, and went and sate down in the
midst of them, and so was comforted with the light
and heat of their sun.[1]

This instinct to dramatise seems to have been spontaneous ; at least in later years, when he came to
write *Pilgrim's Progress*, the allegory bubbled out
of his mind without any conscious effort at creation.
At this time his intellectual struggles appeared as
a great drama in which the three protagonists were
Satan, eager to catch him, God, jealous yet sternly
merciful, and his own soul, very uncertainly struggling
forward.

At the end then of the period of outward reforma-

[1] *Grace Abounding*, §§ 53, 54. Psychologists interpret this dream
differently.

tion Bunyan was at first in a state of complacent self-satisfaction, though constantly harassed by external vexations. If, as is not improbable, he had again looked at the *Plain Man's Pathway* he would have been brought to realise that his state was actually worse than before, for, as Theologus persuades Asunetes in the dialogue, spiritual complacency is itself a most deadly sin.

Meanwhile he had to earn his living, and going to Bedford, he came on these poor women, and was at once impressed, not so much by their words as by their obvious happiness, for they evidently possessed some grace which he certainly did not. He went again and fell in with their way of thought, so that for the time his whole mind was bent on eternity. But there were two disturbing experiences.

There was a young man in our town, to whom my heart before was knit more than to any other ; but he being a most wicked creature for cursing and swearing, and whoring, I now shook him off, and forsook his company. But about a quarter of a year after I had left him, I met him in a certain lane, and asked him how he did ; he, after his old swearing and mad way, answered, he was well. " But, Harry," said I, " why do you swear and curse thus ? What will become of you, if you die in this condition ? " He answered me in a great chafe, " What would the Devil do for company, if it were not for such as I am ? "

30

The second experience was when a poor man who had formerly given him much encouragement turned Ranter, " and gave himself up to all manner of filthiness, especially uncleanness. He would also deny that there was a God, Angel, or Spirit; And would laugh at all exhortations to sobriety. When I laboured to rebuke his wickedness, he would laugh the more, and pretend that he had gone through all religions, and could never light on the right, till now. He told me also, that in a little time, I should see all professors turn to the ways of the Ranters. Wherefore, abominating those cursed principles, I left his company forthwith, and became to him as great a stranger as I had been before a familiar." [1] The poor man's words afterwards gave Bunyan much torture.

He now betook himself once more to the Bible, and especially the " Epistles of the Apostle St. Paul," wherein he read, " To one is given by the Spirit the word of wisdom; to another the word of knowledge by the same Spirit; and to another, faith," etc. (1 Cor. xii). Musing on this text, he realised that he wanted knowledge and understanding, but at least he had faith. But the phrase kept running in his mind, " But how if you want faith indeed ? But how can you tell if you have faith ? " The solution which first suggested itself was to attempt some miracle. Being between Elstow and Bedford

[1] *Grace Abounding,* §§ 43, 44.

he thought of commanding the puddles in the horse-pads, " Be dry," and the dry places " Be you the puddles." Fortunately this experiment was frustrated by the thought that if it failed then he would prove himself faithless, and so be lost utterly.

The next difficulties presented themselves in these words : " But how if the day of grace should now be past and gone ? " " How can you tell you are elected ? And what if you should not ? How then ? " To these questions he could not at first find any answer, except the reflection, " For it is neither in him that willeth, nor in him that runneth ; but in God that sheweth mercy " ; if God had not elected him, there was no question of his being saved. This perplexity was for a time resolved by another text which his mind threw up, " Look at the generations of old and see : did ever any trust in the Lord and was confounded ? " " At which," says he, " I was greatly lightened, and encouraged in my soul ; for thus at that very instant, it was expounded to me : Begin at the beginning of Genesis, and read to the end of the Revelations, and see if you can find that there was ever any that trusted in the Lord, and was confounded. So coming home I presently went to my Bible, to see if I could find that saying, not doubting but to find it presently ; for it was so fresh, and with such strength and comfort on my spirit, that I was as if it talked with me." [1] But it was a

[1] *Grace Abounding,* § 63.

year before he could find the text, and then in the Apocrypha.

Meanwhile another problem arose : " How if the good people of Bedford were all that God would save in those parts ? " The solution was found in " compel them to come in, that my house may be filled ; *and yet there is room*." But, he reflected, none but those who are effectually called inherit the Kingdom of Heaven ; and he had not been called.

About this time he began to open his heart to the poor people of Bedford, who told their minister, Mr. Gifford, of his state. This was the decisive step in Bunyan's conversion, for he found in Gifford what he had been seeking all this while, a sympathetic confessor, a man of better education than himself, who had passed along the same way, and had made a map of the route as he went.

John Gifford had passed through more remarkable experiences than Bunyan. He was in 1648 a Major in the Royalist Army, and had taken a prominent part in the rising in Kent. After the Royalists had been defeated at Maidstone, he, with eleven other officers, was condemned to death, but the night before execution his sister, on coming to visit him, found the sentries sound asleep and persuaded him to escape. For three days he lay hid in a ditch ; thence he made his way to London and ultimately to Bedford, where he was quite unknown. There he set up as a physician, but "abode still very vile and debauched in life, being a great drinker, gamster, swearer, &c." After frequent losses at play, he resolved to give it up, but still persisted until one night, having lost about £15, "it put him into a rage, and he thought many desperate thoughts against God. But while he was looking into one of Mr. Bolton's books something therein took hold upon him and brought him into a great sense of sin, wherein he continued for the space of a month or above. But at last God did so plentifully discover to him by his word the forgiveness of his sins for the sake of Christ, that (as he hath by several of the brethren been heard to say) all his life after, which was about the space of five years, he lost not the light of God's countenance —no, not for an hour, save only about two days before he died." [1]

At first the godly in Bedford were afraid of him, but in the end, after much prayer and consultation, the community at Bedford was founded; "and at length twelve of the holy brethren and sisters began this holy work, viz.: Mr. John Grew and his wife, Mr. John Eston, the elder, Anthony Harrington and his wife, Mr. John Gifford, Sister Coventon, Sister Bosworth, Sister Munnes, Sister Fenn, and Sister Norton, and Sister Spenser; all ancient and grave Christians well known one to

[1] The full account is given in the opening pages of the *Church Book*.

another, Sister Norton being the youngest." And these were the " poor women of Bedford " that brought Bunyan to Gifford, whom they had elected to be their first pastor.

Bunyan was still a very long way from peace of mind; Gifford's standard of grace was high, and Bunyan was the more acutely conscious of his own shortcomings. Besides, he noticed that the true professors were themselves much dejected by outward losses, or when afflicted in the conscience were more concerned with easing the mind than obtaining pardon from sin. Man, he reflected, was the most noble of all creatures in the visible world; but by sin he had made himself the most ignoble. The birds, beasts and fishes were blessed in their condition, for they had not a sinful nature; they were not obnoxious to the wrath of God; they were not to go to hell-fire after death.

In this state of mind he continued until he heard a sermon wherein the preacher, choosing his text from the Song of Solomon—" Behold thou art fair, my love; behold thou art fair "—took the words " my love " as his subject; " poor tempted soul, when thou art assaulted and afflicted with temptations, and the hidings of God's grace, yet think on these two words, *my love*, still." As Bunyan was going home the words began to kindle in his spirit, " Thou art my love, thou art my dove," twenty times together. . . . " But is it true ? But is it true ? " . . .

" He wist not that it was true, which was done
unto him of the Angel." Then he began to give
place to the word which over and over again made
this joyful sound within his soul. " Thou art my
love, thou art my love, and nothing shall separate
me from my love." And with that came into his
mind : " Nor height, nor depth, nor any other creature, shall be able to separate us from the love of
God, which is in Christ Jesus our Lord."

This peace of mind was brief, for the next text
which sounded in his ears was " Simon, Simon,
behold, Satan hath desired to have you," and so
insistent was the echo of the words that the word
" Simon " seemed to come from without, as if
someone had called after him half a mile behind.

There succeeded another period of storm, fiercer
than anything which he had yet experienced. In
all his doubts and questionings hitherto Bunyan
had at least been convinced, without question, that
the Scriptures were indeed the very word and voice
of God. Now arose a new doubt whether there
was in truth a God or Christ, whether the Holy
Scriptures were not rather a fable and cunning story.
Might not the Turks' scriptures to prove their Ma-
homet the saviour be as good ? And how could it
be that so many ten thousands, in so many countries
and kingdoms, should be without the knowledge
of the right way to heaven (if there were indeed a
heaven) and that we only, who live in a corner of

the earth, should be alone blessed therewith? Everyone thinks his own religion rightest; both Jews and Moors and Pagans; and how if all our faith, and Christ, and scriptures should be but a "think so" too?

Against these insinuations he set some sentences from Paul; but then Paul also might have been a subtle and cunning man, who had given himself up to deceive with strong delusions. These doubts may have been spontaneous, but it is as likely that they were the arguments of the opposer in some religious debate. Logic based on reason failing to carry conviction, Bunyan was forced back on intuition, which refused to accept these suggestions of the Tempter.

Nevertheless Bunyan's hold on faith was not a little shaken; prayer became difficult, and any little thing would distract his attention; God seemed distant and derisive of his efforts. But once more hope returned; "For he hath made him to be sin for us who knew no sin, that we might be made the righteousness of God in him." . . . "If God be for us, who can be against us." . . . "Because I live, ye shall live also"; and especially with these words, "Forasmuch then as the children are partakers of flesh and blood, he also himself likewise took part of the same, that through death he might destroy him that had the power of death, that is,

¹ § *Grace Abounding,* § 116.

the Devil; and deliver those who, through fear of
death, were all their lifetime subject to bondage"
(Heb. ii. 14, 15).

This record of Bunyan's mental state may give
the wrong impression that he was entirely an introspective person, who communed much with himself,
after the manner of William Wordsworth. Most
of his struggles seem to have occurred while he was
walking alone either between Elstow and Bedford,
or elsewhere on his business; but he was a man of
strong personal affections, who needed and made
friends, and whilst he observed the stirrings of his
own mind he watched his neighbours as closely,
comparing their mentality and conduct with his own.
He had, in fact, a profound knowledge of the
workings of the human heart.

The community in Bedford was founded on the
principle of "*faith in Christ and holiness of life*, without
respect to this or that circumstance or opinion in
outward and circumstantial things. By which means
grace and faith was encouraged, Love and Amity
maintained, disputings and occasion to janglings
and unprofitable questions avoided, and many that
were weak in faith confirmed in the blessing of
eternal life."[1] John Gifford based his religion
on intuitive belief in God and not on a particular
interpretation of Scripture, and in his preaching he
constantly warned his hearers not to take any truth

[1] *Church Book*, f. 2.

on trust, but to cry mightily to God to convince them of its reality. It was this conviction which Bunyan especially needed to guard him from putting too much trust in particular texts.

Meanwhile, though he was gradually drawing towards peace of mind the struggles continued. Certain landmarks stand out to mark the stages. The Quakers, for instance, were always particularly obnoxious to Bunyan, because of their doctrines; they taught, as he maintained:

1. That the Holy Scriptures were not the Word of God.

2. That every man in the World had the Spirit of Christ, Grace, Faith, &c.

3. That Christ Jesus, as crucified, and dying sixteen hundred years ago, did not satisfie Divine Justice for the sins of his people.

4. That Christ's Flesh and Blood was within the Saints.

5. That the Bodies of the Good and Bad that are buried in the Churchyard, shall not arise again.

6. That the resurrection is past with good men already.

7. That the Man Jesus, that was crucified between two thieves, on Mount Calvary, in the Land of Canaan, by Jerusalem, was not ascended up above the starry Heavens.

8. That he should not, even the same Jesus that died by the hand of the Jews, come again at the last day; and, as Man, judge all Nations, &c.

It did Bunyan good to refute their doctrines from the Scriptures because it led him to formulate and order his own beliefs.

The next stage was the accidental discovery of an old copy of Martin Luther's *Commentary on the Galatians*.

Meanwhile, the pendulum in Bunyan's mind was beginning to swing wider; but between ecstasies and the reactions of despair he was finding balance. His path, though still uncertain, was in the direction of the little congregation at Bedford. There were still terrible struggles, some of them caused by odd sayings and phrases which throbbed in his head like the pulsations in a septic wound, others arising from the self-torment of a religious mind wrenching texts from their proper surroundings and setting them off one against another.

The minds of most men are inhabited by two separate beings or voices; the one creative and inspiring and active, the other critical, negative, and restraining. Blake called them imagination and reason, regarding the creator as the emanation of God, and reason the restrainer as the voice of the devil. Most religious men, however, reverse the process, and call the creator lust, a creature all too readily fluttered by the temptations of the world, the flesh, and the devil; while they exalt the critic into the Voice of God breathing through the conscience. And indeed the history of human thought is largely the story of the struggle between these two. In Christianity itself the two sides are expressed by Jesus and Paul; Jesus, substituting a creative life of " thou shalt love thy neighbour as thyself " for the old negations of the Decalogue, condemned one sin only as unforgivable, the sin against the Holy Ghost. To Paul, Christianity was more negative, and his list of the unforgivable sins was large—" Adultery, fornication, uncleanness, lasciviousness, idolatry, witchcraft, hatred, variance, emulations, wrath, strife, sedition, heresies, envyings, murders, drunkenness, revellings, and such like : . . . they which do such things shall not inherit the kingdom of God " (Gal. v. 19–21).

The divine humanity of Jesus made very little impression on Bunyan ; he took Paul as his model ; and to him—at least in the early days of his conversion—Christ's chief importance in the divine scheme of the universe was that his body contained enough blood to satisfy even Jehovah as a sacrifice for the sins of mankind.

The argument between critic and creator is a familiar process in the mind, though it takes different forms according to the individual. In the majority of educated persons neither is very distinct, and both work together, the critic often following the creator and devising reasons to justify desire. The less educated a man is, the more usually will he be conscious of his mental processes, and when obliged to think out a problem he will argue after the manner of Launcelot Gobbo.

" Budge," says the fiend; " budge not," says my conscience : " Conscience," say I, " you counsel well ; fiend," say I, " you counsel well : to be ruled by my conscience I should stay with the Jew my master, who (God bless the mark !) is a kind of devil; and to run away from the Jew I should be ruled by the fiend, who, saving your reverence, is the devil himself. Certainly, the Jew is the very devil incarnal : and, in my conscience, my conscience is a kind of hard conscience, to offer to counsel me to stay with the Jew : The fiend gives the more friendly counsel : I will run, fiend ; my heels are at your commandment, I will run." [1]

In a very sensitive person, who has not been trained (or dragooned) by education to control the mind, the duality of critic and creator is sometimes so intense that their voices become audible not only to the inner ear but sometimes almost to the outer ear as well. And so with Bunyan ; but with him the creator allied himself at this time with the Tempter, and the critic was hard beset to find adequate answers in this audible debate. Besides, the creator used rhythmic incantations which soon upset Bunyan's mental balance. A good example of this kind of textual warfare is the great debate in his mind over selling Christ.

[1] *Merchant of Venice*, II, ii.

THE CONVERT

The Tempter came upon me again, and that with a more grievous and dreadful temptation than before.

And that was, to sell and part with this most blessed Christ, to exchange him for the things of this life, for anything. The temptation lay upon me for the space of a year, and did follow me so continually, that I was not rid of it one day in a month ; no, not sometimes one hour in many days together, unless when I was asleep.

And though in my judgment I was persuaded, that those who were once effectually in Christ (as I hoped, through his Grace, I had seen myself) could never lose him for ever—(For the land shall not be sold for ever, for the land is mine, saith God, Lev. xxv. 23)—yet it was a continual vexation to me, to think that I should have so much as one such thought within me against a Christ, a Jesus, that had done for me as he had done ; and yet then I had almost none others, but such blasphemous ones.

But it was neither my dislike of the thought, nor yet any desire and endeavour to resist it, that in the least did shake or abate the continuation, or force and strength thereof ; for it did always, in almost whatever I thought, intermix itself therewith in such sort that I could neither eat my food, stoop for a pin, chop a stick, or cast mine eye to look on this or that, but still the temptation would come, " Sell Christ for this, or sell Christ for that ; sell him, sell him."

Sometimes it would run in my thoughts, not so little as an hundred times together ; " Sell him, sell him, sell him " ; against which, I may say, for whole hours together, I have been forced to stand as continually leaning and forcing my spirit against it, lest haply, before I were aware, some wicked thought might arise in my heart, that might consent thereto ; and sometimes also the Tempter would make me believe I had consented to it, then should I be as tortured upon a rack for whole days together.

This temptation did put me to such scares, lest I should at some times, I say, consent thereto, and be overcome therewith, that by the very force of my mind, in labouring to gainsay and resist this wickedness, my very body also would be put into action, or motion, by way of pushing or thrusting with my hands, or elbows ; still answering, as fast as the destroyer said, " sell him " ; " I will not, I will not, I will not, I will not ; no, not for thousands, thousands, thousands of worlds." Thus reckoning, lest I should, in the midst of these assaults, set too low a value of him, even until I scarce well knew where I was, or how to be composed again.

At these seasons he would not let me eat my food at quiet ; but, forsooth, when I was set at the table, at my meat, I must go hence to pray ; I must leave my food now, and just now ; so counterfeit holy also would this Devil be. When I was thus tempted, I should say in myself, " Now I am at my meat, let me make an end." " No," said he, " you must do it now, or you will displease God, and despise Christ." Wherefore I was much afflicted with these things ; and because of the sinfulness of my nature (imagining that these things were impulses from God) I should deny to do it, as if I denied God ; and then should I be as guilty because I did not obey a temptation

44

of the Devil, as if I had broken the Law of God indeed.

But to be brief, one morning as I did lie in my bed, I was, as at other times, most fiercely assaulted with this temptation, to sell, and part with Christ ; the wicked suggestion still running in my mind, " Sell him, sell him, sell him, sell him, sell him," as fast as a man could speak. Against which also, in my mind, as at other times, I answered, " No, no, not for thousands, thousands, thousands," at least twenty times together. But at last, after much striving, even until I was almost out of breath, I felt this thought pass through my heart, " Let him go, if he will " ; and I thought also that I felt my heart freely consent thereto. Oh, the diligence of Satan ! Oh, the desperateness of Man's heart ! [1]

Critic Reason, however, after this heavy defeat at last found a decisive answer : " ' The blood of Christ remits all guilt.' At this I made a stand in my spirit : with that this word took hold upon me, ' The blood of Jesus Christ his Son cleanseth us from all sin.' "

There were other struggles as great, but with each the defeat of the Tempter became easier as the critic learned to handle his weapons more freely. Thus the Tempter suggested—

That neither the mercy of God, nor yet the blood of Christ, did at all concern me, nor could they help me for my sin ; therefore it was in vain to pray.

[1] *Grace Abounding,* §§ 133-40.

45

" Yet," thought I, " I will pray." " But," said the Tempter, " your sin is unpardonable." " Well," said I, " I will pray." " It is to no boot," said he. " Yet," said I, " I will pray." So I went to prayer to God ; and while I was at prayer, I uttered words to this effect, " Lord, Satan tells me, that neither thy mercy nor Christ's blood is sufficient to save my soul: Lord, shall I honour thee most, by believing thou wilt and canst ? or him, by believing thou neither wilt nor canst ? Lord, I would fain honour thee, by believing thou wilt and canst."

And as I was thus before the Lord, that Scripture fastened on my heart, " O man, great is thy faith " (Mat. xv. 28), even as if one had clapped me on the back, as I was on my knees before God. Yet I was not able to believe this, that this was a prayer of faith, till almost six months after ; for I could not think that I had faith, or that there should be a word for me to act faith on ; therefore I should still be, as sticking in the jaws of desperation, and went mourning up and down, in a sad condition."

At another time the question propounded was, Whether the blood of Christ was sufficient to save his soul ?

In which doubt I continued, from morning, till about seven or eight at night ; and at last, when I was, as it were, quite worn out with fear, lest it should not lay hold on me, these words did sound suddenly within my heart, " He is able." But methought, this word *Able*, was spoke loud unto me ; it showed such a great word, it seemed to be writ in great letters,

46

and gave such a justle to my fear and doubt, I mean, for the time it tarried with me, which was about a day, as I never had from that, all my life, either before or after that. (Heb. vii. 25.) [1]

After further trials, temptations, and questionings, Bunyan formally applied to walk in the order and ordinances of Christ with the community at Bedford and was duly admitted; he was the nineteenth person to join the " people of God."

The Tempter was foiled and defeated, but he still gave trouble, for this new step led Bunyan to further examination of his past life and especially his deadness in holy things, his want of love to God, his ways, and people. He even went so far as to blaspheme the people. But the arguments of Paul strengthened him once more, and soon afterwards the whole series of mental conflicts reached a triumphant climax. He had been in a condition of spiritual weariness for some three or four days, and as he was sitting by the fire he suddenly felt this word to sound in his heart, " I must go to Jesus."

At this my former darkness and atheism fled away, and the blessed things of Heaven were set within my view. While I was on this sudden thus over-taken with surprize, " Wife," said I, " is there ever such a Scripture, I must go to Jesus ? " She said she could not tell; therefore I sat musing still to

[1] *Grace Abounding,* §§ 200, 201, 203.

see if I could remember such a place ; I had not sat above two or three minutes, but that came bolting in upon me, " And to an innumerable company of Angels " ; and withal, Hebrews the twelfth, about the Mount Sion, was set before mine eyes (Heb. xii. 22, 23, 24).

Then with joy I told my wife, " O now I know, I know ! " But that night was a good night to me, I never had but few better ; I longed for the company of some of God's people, that I might have imparted unto them what God had showed me. Christ was a precious Christ to my Soul that night, I could scarce lie in my bed for joy, and peace, and triumph, through Christ ; this great glory did not continue upon me until morning, yet the twelfth of the Author to the Hebrews (Heb. xii. 22, 23) was a blessed Scripture to me for many days together after this.

The words are these, " Ye are come unto Mount Sion, and unto the City of the living God, the Heavenly Jerusalem, and to an innumerable company of angels, to the general assembly and church of the firstborn which are written in Heaven, to God the judge of all, and to the spirits of just men made perfect, and to Jesus the Mediator of the New Covenant, and to the blood of sprinkling, that speaketh better things than that of Abel." Through this blessed sentence, the Lord led me over and over, first to this word, and then to that, and showed me wonderful glory in every one of them. These words also have oft since this time been great refreshment to my Spirit. Blessed be God for having mercy on me.[1]

[1] *Grace Abounding*, §§ 263–5.

THE CONVERT

After such an intensity of emotion the spirit
becomes first molten, and then hardened to a kind of
clinker.   Henceforward, though doubts and problems
in plenty still confronted him, his mind was set ; he
was convinced that the Scriptures, or rather his
interpretation of the Scriptures, was true ; it remained for him to regulate his life rigidly to their
standards.

D

THE PRISONER

CHAPTER II

IN 1653, under Cromwell's Broad Church Policy, Gifford was presented to the living of St. John's Church by the Town Council of Bedford. Bunyan was received into his community in 1655, and soon afterwards he went to live in Bedford. Gifford died in the following September and was succeeded by John Burton, who, after some months of controversy, was also appointed to the vacant living. The records in the *Church Book* begin with a meeting on 24th May 1656.

Bunyan had already been noticed by his fellows and had spoken twice at their meetings.[1] Accordingly, when some of the brethren went into the country to preach, he was asked to accompany them. Some months before this his controversies with the Quakers had led Bunyan into print with his first book, *Some Gospel Truths Opened*; to which the Quakers issued a reply, putting certain doctrinal questions to him. Bunyan retorted with *A Vindication of Gospel Truths Opened*. The vigorous combativeness of these two pamphlets shows that he had completely subdued his spiritual diffidence. Bunyan's name first occurs in the *Church Book* on 28th June 1657, when it was agreed that he should go with Brother Child

[1] *Grace Abounding*, §§ 266, 267.

and Brother John Fenn to friend Stratton, junior, of Stratton.

On the 27th of September, with three others, he was nominated for trial as a deacon, but another was chosen in his place, " Bro. Bunyan being taken off by preaching of the Gospell." He was now one of their leaders. On 25th March 1658 he was instructed with Brother Child to visit Brother Skelton, and with Brother Samuel Fenn to visit Sister Chamberlain ; but he did not, and at the next meeting (29th of May) he was reminded of his neglect and " required to take care of it against the next meeting."

He was now preaching regularly, and with great success ; " which when the country understood, they came in to hear the Word by hundreds, and that from all parts, though upon sundry and divers accounts."

Several important events happened in this year 1658 outside the parish church of Bedford, where Bunyan's brethren in Christ held their meetings.

Sir Thomas Browne, physician of Norwich, published a book entitled *Enquiries into Vulgar Errors*. It was not, of course, in any sense an attack on the authenticity of the Scriptures ; still, when a man of sceptical notions begins to demonstrate that men have the same number of ribs as women, or that the date of the beginning of the world is not exactly known, then the foundations of the doctrine of Law and Grace show some faint cracks.

THE PRISONER

On the 3rd of September Oliver Cromwell, Lord Protector, passed over to await the Last Judgment. Three days later the *Publick Intelligencer* officially announced his death, and amongst the advertisements of books newly published appeared *A Few Sighs from Hell, or the Groans of a Damned Soul*, by John Bunyan.

This book is based on one of his sermons on the parable of Dives and Lazarus, and is a good example of his first style of preaching.

Now this part of my work I fulfilled with great sense, for the terrors of the law, and guilt for my transgressions lay heavy on my conscience. I preached what I felt, what I smartingly did feel, even that under which my poor soul did groan and tremble to astonishment." [1]

His conversion was still fresh in him, and the power of the sermon lies in the vivid, graphic words of one who has acutely experienced what he describes.

At this time Bunyan's trade and humble origin were being thrown in his teeth. " J. G.," who commends the book to the reader at some length, justifies the outward condition and former employment of the author, and the smallness of his human learning, by the reminder that Jesus also came from a humble trade. Bunyan himself ends his preface with the words, " I am thine, if thou be not ashamed

[1] *Grace Abounding,* § 276.

to own me, because of my low and contemptible descent in the world "—a sentence which in later editions he changed to " I am thine to serve in the Lord Jesus." The choice of text and subject was therefore not an inappropriate hint to those of better birth and education that in another world carnal values are liable to be reversed.

The general design of the sermon is familiar. First the text (Luke xvi. 19–31) is taken as a whole, and then commented upon verse by verse, and phrase by phrase ; then the lessons to be deduced are applied. As a whole, the book is over-long, and is swelled out with unnecessary repetitions, yet it abounds in good passages which illustrate the technique of Bunyan's early preachings.

Hell at all times had greatly fascinated him, and by constant brooding he had formed a most vivid impression, visual and mental, of its torments. There, he says, the sinner shall have nothing but a company of damned souls with an innumerable company of devils to keep company with him.

While thou art in this world, the very thought of the devils appearing to thee makes thy flesh to tremble, and thine hair ready to stand upright on thy head. But O ! what wilt thou do, when not only the supposition of the devils appearing, but the real society of all the devils in hell will be with thee howling and roaring, screeching and roaring in such a hideous manner, that thou wilt be even at thy wits' end, and be ready to run stark mad again for anguish and torment ? [1]

Then there is the bodily torment of hell. The words of the text—" Send Lazarus that he may dip the tip of his finger in water and cool my tongue " —remind him of his own most erring member, and he digresses for a little to consider the tongue in a passage which is worth noting for its elaborate artistry.

Why is it said, " Let him dip the tip of his finger in water, and cool my tongue " ? Because that, as the several members in the body have their share in sin, and committing of that, so the several members of the body shall at that time be punished for the same. Therefore, when Christ is admonishing his disciples, that they should not turn aside from him, and that they should rather fear and dread the power of their God than any other power, he saith, " Fear him, therefore, that can cast both body and soul into hell " (Luke xii. 4). And again, " Fear him which is able to destroy both soul and body in hell " (Matt. x. 28). Here is not one member only, but all the body, the whole body of which the hands, feet, eyes, ears, and tongue are members. And I am persuaded, that though this may be judged carnal by some now, yet it will appear to be a truth then, to the greater misery of those who shall be forced to undergo that which God, in his just judgment, shall inflict upon them. O then they will cry, " One

[1] *Works*, iii, 684.

dram of ease for my cursing, swearing, lying, jeering tongue. Some ease for my bragging, braving, flattering, threatening, dissembling tongue." Now men can let their tongues run at random, as we used to say ; now they will be apt to say, " Our tongues are our own, who shall control them ? " (Ps. xii. 4). But then they will be in another mind. Then, " O that I might have a little ease for my deceitful tongue ? " Methinks sometimes to consider how some men do let their tongues run at random, it makes me marvel. Surely they do not think they shall be made to give an account for their offending with their tongue. Did they but think they shall be made to give an account to him who is ready to judge the quick and the dead, surely they would be more wary of, and have more regard unto their tongue.

" The tongue," saith James, " is an unruly evil, full of deadly poison " ; " it setteth on fire the course of nature, and it is set on fire of hell " (Jas. ii). The tongue, how much mischief will it stir up in a very little time ! How many blows and wounds doth it cause ! How many times doth it, as James saith, curse man ! How oft is the tongue made the con-veyer of that hellish poison that is in the heart, both to the dishonour of God, the hurt of its neighbours, and the utter ruin of its own soul ! And do you think the Lord will sit still, as I may say, and let thy tongue run as it lists, and yet never bring you to an account for the same ? No, stay. The Lord will not always keep silence, but will reprove thee, and set thy sins in order before thine eyes, O sinner. Yea, and thy tongue, together with the rest of thy members, shall be tormented for sinning. And I say, I am very confident, that though this be made light of now, yet the time is coming when many poor souls will rue the day that ever they did speak with a tongue. O, will one say, that I should so disregard my tongue ! O that I, when I said so and so, had before bitten off my tongue ! That I had been born without a tongue ! my tongue, my tongue, a little water to cool my tongue, for I am tormented in this flame ; even in that flame that my tongue, together with the rest of my members, by sinning, have brought me to. Poor souls now will let their tongues say anything for a little profit, for two-pence or three-pence gain. But, O what a grief will this be at that day when they, together with their tongue, must smart for that which they by their tongues have done while they were in this world. Then, you that love your souls, look to your tongues, lest you bind yourselves down so fast to hell with the sins of your tongues, that you will never be able to get loose again to all eternity. " For by thy words thou shalt be condemned," if thou have not a care of thy tongue. For " I say unto you, That every idle word that men shall speak, they shall give account thereof in the day of judgment " (Matt. xii. 36).[1]

In this passage he begins on the level of conversation, with the preacher's question and answer, " Why the tongue ? " Thence he rises into rhetoric, piling up the epithets, dropping for a moment at the end of the paragraph, but soaring again with the quotation

[1] *Works*, iii, 688–9.

from James to reach his climax in the words, " For
I say unto you that every idle word that men shall
speak, they shall give account thereof in the day of
judgment."

The digression is linked to the main argument by
the one word " tongue " (which Bunyan probably
pronounced " tong "), and this word, repeated
almost at even intervals, clangs solemnly with the
insistence of a funeral bell. If this effect is uncon-
scious it is the more remarkable.

Repetition is common in Bunyan's sermons ; he
had suffered himself from the reverberation of words
and rhythms, and as it was his habit to measure
others by his own standard, he tried to induce the
same effect in them by the same means. He does
not confine repetition to phrases, but uses it on a
larger scale, circling round his subject, and at each
revolution seeing it from some slightly different
aspect : for instance, at verse 26—" besides all this,
between us and you there is a great gulf fixed "—
he comes back to hell and its torments, which are now
expressed in more homely terms.

It is true, I spoke enough before to break thine
heart asunder ; but " beside all this," there lie and
swim in flames for ever. These words, " Beside
all this," are terrible words indeed. I will give you
the scope of them in a similitude. Set the case you
should take a man, and tie him to a stake, and with
red-hot pinchers, pinch off his flesh by little pieces
60

for two or three years together, and at last, when the poor man cries out for ease and help, the tormentors answer, "Nay, but beside all this, you must be handled worse. We will serve you thus these twenty years together, and after that we will fill your mangled body full of scalding lead, or run you through with a red-hot spit"; would not this be lamentable? Yet this is but a flea-biting to the sorrow of those that go to hell; for if a man were served so there would, ere it were long, be an end of him. But he that goes to hell shall suffer ten thousand times worse torments than these, and yet shall never be quite dead under them. There they shall be ever whining, pining, weeping, mourning, ever tormented without ease; and yet never dissolved into nothing. If the biggest devil in hell might pull thee all to pieces, and rend thee small as dust, and dissolve thee into nothing, thou wouldst count this a mercy. But here thou mayst lie and fry, scorch and broil, and burn for ever. For ever, that is a long while, and yet it must be so long. "Depart from me, ye cursed," saith Christ, "into everlasting fire," into the fire that burns for ever, "prepared for the devil and his angels" (Matt. xxv. 41). O! thou that wast loath to foul thy foot if it were but dirty, or did but rain; thou that wast loath to come out of the chimney-corner, if the wind did but blow a little cold; and wast loath to go half-a-mile, yea, half-a-furlong to hear the word of God, if it were but a little dark; thou that wast loath to leave a few vain companions, to edify thy soul; thou shalt have fire enough, thou shalt have night enough, and evil company enough, thy bellyfull, if thou miss of

Jesus Christ; and beside all this, thou shalt have them for ever, and for ever.[1]

The book also gives some valuable light on Bunyan's reading in his unregenerate days, in a remark put into the mouth of Dives, who in his pride and ignorance had rejected the words of the preacher:

"I remember he alleged many a Scripture, but those I valued not; the Scriptures, thought I, what are they? A dead letter, a little ink and paper, of three or four shillings price. Alas! What is the Scripture? Give me a ballad, a news-book, *George on horseback*, or *Bevis of Southampton*; give me some book that teaches curious arts, that tells of old fables; but for the Holy Scriptures I cared not." [2]

Towards the end of 1658 difference of opinion arose between the congregation and others in communion with them, and on the 30th of October Brother Burton, their pastor, with Brothers Grew, Harrington, Whiteman, and Bunyan were instructed to meet together and "to consider of some things that may conduce to love and unity amongst us all." The question was still being debated in the following February, and it was agreed that Bunyan, Grew, and Harrington should meet the brethren of the other churches about the matter. After this Bunyan's name does not reappear in the book for fifteen

---

[1] *Works*, iii, 693–4.   [2] *Ibid.*, p. 711.

months; the time was presumably occupied with writing and preaching.

About this time Bunyan's first wife died, leaving him with four small children to whom he was much attached, and especially to his daughter Mary; she was blind. After a short interval he married again.

Bunyan continued to preach in the style of *Sighs from Hell* for two years, " crying out against men's sins, and their fearful state because of them."

After which [he continues[1]] the Lord came in upon my own Soul with some staid peace and comfort through Christ; for he did give me many sweet discoveries of his Blessed Grace through him; Wherefore now I altered in my preaching, for still I preached what I saw and felt; now therefore I did much labour to hold forth Jesus Christ in all his Offices, Relations, and Benefits unto the World, and did strive also to discover, to condemn, and remove those false supports and props on which the World doth both lean, and by them fall and perish. On these things also I staid as long as on the other.[2]

The discourses of this period were published in 1659: *The Doctrine of the Law and Grace Unfolded.* The change of style, outlook, and mental state is obvious; in *Sighs from Hell* Bunyan preached in a frenzy, driving his hearers before him as a shepherd hurries his flock from an approaching avalanche. In the *Doctrine of the Law and Grace Unfolded,* the

---

[1] In *Grace Abounding.*   [2] *Ibid.,* § 278.

frenzy has evaporated; the book is long-winded, tedious, and complacent, expanding the dialectics of Paul on the Old and the New Covenants into an interminable argument on Law and Grace. Bunyan had reached a second stage in his conversion; his enthusiasm was cooling off. The battle being over, he began to concern himself with the red tape of Christianity, tracing the tedious ways of art which " professors " follow in peaceful times.

The argument of the book, set out under headings, sections, and sub-sections, is based on the text, " For ye are not under the law, but under grace " (Romans vi. 14). Bunyan divides his discourse into two main parts, the first considering the Law, or the " Covenant of Works "; the second the new Covenant of Grace, made with Christ.

The Covenant of Works is the law delivered on Mount Sinai in the two tables of stone; this law, however, was anticipated in the commandment originally given to Adam. No one living under it has any chance of salvation, because " Cursed is everyone that continueth not in ALL things which are written in the book of the law to do them." The law condemns not only words and actions, but even the secret thoughts of the heart; so that if a man has refrained from speaking any word that is evil, yet if there has chanced to pass but one vain thought through his heart but once in all his lifetime, the law takes hold of it, accuses and also will condemn him for it. God gave the law that sin might abound and for his own self-protection, lest at the Day of Judgment any of the condemned should plead, " Lord, why am I thus condemned ? I did not know it was sin." Nor can the Gentiles and barbarians, who have not received the light, plead ignorance, because they have the law of works in them by nature, that is, in their consciences. All this God has ordained to magnify his own holiness and justice.

On the other hand, the people of God are not under the law of Works, but under Grace ; Grace being the free love of God in Christ to sinners, by virtue of the New Covenant, which delivers them from the power of sin and the condemnations of the Old Covenant. This Grace is the free gift of God and does not depend on the righteousness of the saint, " God having no first eye to what they would do, or should do, for the obtaining of the same." The sinner is thus converted by God, and not by his own efforts. This conception of conversion Bunyan justifies with " a word of experience " wherein he anticipates *Grace Abounding*. The Lord, finding him in a condition of sin, had made his conscience very tender, and then, when he was overwhelmed with the load of his sins, applied the blood spilt at Mount Calvary, to his immediate comfort and peace.

God's grace is unchangeable, and those to whom he gives it are made brethren with Jesus Christ,

E   65

members of his flesh and his bones, the spouse of
this Lord Jesus.

But there are certain obvious objections to this
doctrine. The saints, after the profession of the
gospel, sometimes fall off again ; how then ? The
answer is that these were not true saints, as no true
saint will ever fall off; he dare not, because he sees
hell-fire prepared for those that sin.

There are even worse objections, which are labelled
as " hell-bred." The first is, that if Christ has by
grace made men free of the law of works, then they
may sin, and sin again, because Christ has already
satisfied God for their sins. These quibbles Bunyan
rejects with fury : although God's covenant is
immutable and unchangeable, yet he has already
anticipated these wretches in such a way that they
cannot go to heaven unless he forswear himself. He
has sworn, and in his wrath, that they shall never
enter into his rest. If Christ will not serve their
turns, the Devil shall have them, to scald, fry, and
burn them in hell.

The book concludes with a picture of the last judgment :

Thou shalt also be lovingly received and tenderly
embraced of him at that day, when Christ hath
thousands of gallant saints, as old Abraham, Isaac,
Jacob, David, Isaiah, Jeremiah, together with all
the prophets, and apostles, and martyrs, attending

66

on him; together with many thousands of glittering angels ministering before him; besides, when the ungodly shall appear there with their pale faces, with their guilty consciences, and trembling souls, that would then give thousands and ten thousands of worlds, if they had so many, if they could enjoy but one loving look from Christ. I say, then, then shalt thou have the hand of Christ reached to thee kindly to receive thee, saying, Come, thou blessed, step up hither; thou wast willing to leave all for me, and now will I give all to thee; here is a throne, a crown, a kingdom, take them; thou wast not ashamed of me when thou wast in the world among my enemies, and now will not I be ashamed of thee before thine enemies, but will, in the view of all these devils and damned reprobates, promote thee to honour and dignity. "Come, ye blessed of my Father, inherit the kingdom prepared for you from the foundation of the world." Thou shalt see that those who have served me in truth shall lose nothing by the means. No; but ye shall be as pillars in my temple, and inheritors of my glory, and shall have place to walk in among my saints and angels (Zech. iii. 7). O! who would not be in this condition? Who would not be in this glory? It will be such a soul-ravishing glory, that I am ready to think the whole reprobate world will be ready to run mad, to think that they should miss of it (Deut. xxviii. 34). Then will the vilest drunkard, swearer, liar, and unclean person willingly cry, "Lord, Lord, open to us," yet be denied of entrance; and thou in the meantime embraced, entertained, made welcome, have a fair mitre set upon thy head, and clothed with immortal glory (Zech. iii. 5). O, therefore, let all this move thee, and be of weight upon thy soul to close in with Jesus, this tender-hearted Jesus. And if yet, for all what I have said, thy sins do still stick with thee, and thou findest thy hellish heart loath to let them go, think with thyself in this manner —Shall I have my sins and lose my soul? Will they do me any good when Christ comes? Would not heaven be better to me than my sins? and the company of God, Christ, saints, and angels, be better than the company of Cain, Judas, Balaam, with the devils in the furnace of fire? Canst thou now that readest or hearest these lines turn thy back, and go on in thy sins? Canst thou set so light of heaven, of God, of Christ, and the salvation of thy poor, yet precious soul? Canst thou hear of Christ, his bloody sweat and death, and not be taken with it, and not be grieved for it, and also converted by it? If so, I might lay thee down several considerations to stir thee up to mend thy pace towards heaven ; but I shall not ; there is enough written already to leave thy soul without excuse, and to bring thee down with a vengeance into hell-fire, devouring fire, the lake of fire, eternal, everlasting fire ; O to make thee swim and roll up and down in the flames of the furnace of fire ! [1]

On 25th May 1660 it was agreed by the church meeting that " our brother Bunyan be prepared to speak a word to us at the next church meeting, and that our brother Whiteman fail not to speak to him

[1] *Works*, i, 574–5.

of it." Four days later King Charles the Second entered London. In September Parliament passed the Act for restoring the ejected ministers of the Church of England; in October the liturgy of the Church was ordered to be read in the Bedford churches.

On the 12th of November Bunyan was invited to preach at Samsell by Harlington, some miles south of Bedford.

Mr. Francis Wingate, the local magistrate, heard of it, and immediately issued a warrant for Bunyan's arrest.[1] Bunyan had warning and could have escaped, but he realised that the time had now come for his faith to be put to the test; if he were to run, what would his weak and newly converted brethren think of it? It would be a discouragement to the whole body, and besides the world would suspect worse of him and his profession than he deserved. The meeting was being opened with prayer when the constable entered with the warrant. Bunyan began to comfort his friends, but as the constable and the justice's man were impatient, he left with them. The justice was not at home that day, but a friend stood security, and next morning Bunyan went with the constable, and so to the justice.

Mr. Wingate asked the constable some questions,

[1] For a full account of Bunyan's arrest and examinations see *A Relation of the imprisonment of Mr. John Bunyan*, first published in 1765. It is usually printed as an appendix to *Grace Abounding*.

who assured him that the meeting was not seditious. Then he turned to Bunyan and asked him why he was not content to follow his calling ; for it was against the law for him to act thus. Bunyan answered that his intention was to instruct and counsel people to forsake their sins, and close in with Christ lest they perished miserably ; and he could do this and follow his calling without confusion. Thereupon the magistrate demanded sureties, who were called in and a bond was drawn for his appearance, upon which Wingate said that they were bound to keep Bunyan from preaching or their bonds would be forfeited. But as Bunyan refused to allow this, a *mittimus* was made out for him to be sent to the jail until the quarter sessions.

While the *mittimus* was being prepared Dr. Lindale, " an old enemy to the truth," came in, and a lively and somewhat abusive argument followed in which Bunyan seems to have got the better, for on his opponent saying " You are one of those scribes and pharisees ; for you with a pretence make long prayers to devour widows' houses," Bunyan countered by answering that if the Doctor got no more by praying and preaching than he had done, he would not be so rich as now he was.

As he was just setting out for Bedford with the constable, two of his brethren met him, and desired the constable to stay, whilst they spoke with the magistrate. After a long discourse they returned, saying that if Bunyan would come back with them and say certain words to the magistrate he would be released. He agreed, but without any expectation that much would come of it.

When he came again before the justice a Mr. Foster of Bedford was in the house, who recognised Bunyan by the light of the candle, for it was now dark, and entering into a long conversation, tried to persuade him to submit. But at length, when both Foster and Wingate saw that Bunyan refused to yield, he was sent off to Bedford jail.

A few days later an attempt was made to have him released on bail, and the prisoner was taken before a Mr. Crumpton, a magistrate of Elstow. But when Crumpton saw the *mittimus* he felt that there might be more against Bunyan than was stated in the charge, and was afraid to take any action. So Bunyan was returned to jail.

In January (1661) the quarter sessions were held at Bedford, and Bunyan was indicted as one that " devilishly and perniciously abstained from coming to church to hear divine service and as a common upholder of several unlawful meetings and conventicles to the great disturbance and distraction of the good subjects of this kingdom." The judge was Justice Keeling, who sat with some of the local justices. He began by asking Bunyan whether he came to the parish church to hear divine service ; Bunyan answered that he did not. Thence they passed into an argument on the scriptural authority for the Prayer Book, Bunyan maintaining that the Spirit, not the Book of Common Prayer, taught men how to pray.

The judge then asked Bunyan what he had to say against the Common Prayer Book.

Bunyan replied, " Sir, if you will hear me, I shall lay down my reasons against it."

The judge assented, but added, " Let me give you one caution : take heed of speaking irreverently of the Common Prayer Book ; for, if you do so, you will bring great damage upon yourself."

The other magistrates now began to join in the argument, but on scriptural arguments Bunyan could hold his own with anyone ; and the judge was obliged to admit that he was not so well versed in Scripture as to dispute, remarking that they could not wait upon him any longer, and adding, " Then you confess the indictment, do you not ? "

Bunyan, who had not realised that this was his trial, answered, " This I confess, we have had many meetings together, both to pray God, and to exhort one another, and that we had the sweet comforting presence of the Lord among us for our encouragement ; blessed be his name therefor." But he would not confess himself guilty otherwise.

Then sentence was passed that he should return to prison and there lie for three months ; after which, if he did not submit to go to church and leave his preaching, he would be banished the realm ; and if, after an appointed day, he should be found in the realm without special licence, concluded the judge, " you must stretch by the neck for it."

Three months after his trial, on 3rd April 1661, Mr. Cobb, the clerk of the peace, came to Bunyan to receive his submission according to the law, and a long but friendly argument ensued, Cobb doing his best to find some way out which would not compromise Bunyan's conscience. Their conversation sets out very clearly the fundamental points of difference between the State and the dissenter at this time. Bunyan claimed that the law against private meetings was directed against those who made religion a pretence for sedition. Cobb replied that everyone could make this claim ; those who took part in Venner's insurrection a few months before (which had led to much bloodshed) had made very good pretences. Would it not be possible for Bunyan to refrain from meetings but to exhort his neighbours privately ? In this way he would do much good. Bunyan's answer was that, if he could do good to one, why not to more ? He should do all the good that he could. The law was directed only against those who made a cloak of religion.

Cobb answered that the private meetings were forbidden because this practice was common enough amongst those who made a pretence of religion. Could Bunyan not submit to do as much good as he could in a neighbourly way without such meetings ?

Bunyan replied that the Lord through grace had so blessed his labour that he dared not but exercise the gift which God had given him.

Cobb then tried a new argument. Other men had the gift ; let him come to public assemblies and hear. Besides, how should they know that he had received a gift ? Would he be willing for two indifferent persons to determine the case, and stand by their judgment ?

" Are they infallible ? " Bunyan asked.

" No," said Cobb.

" Then it is possible my judgment may be as good as theirs." He would, however, be judged by Scripture.

Would he be willing to stand to the judgment of the Church of God ? Yes, the Church of God ; the Church's judgment is best expressed in the Scriptures. After further argument about submission to the laws of the nation, he said that he would willingly give anyone the notes of all his sermons, for he sincerely wished to live quietly in his country and to submit to present authority.

Cobb then earnestly pleaded with him to submit himself, and reminded him that the Scripture said " the powers that be are ordained of God " ; the King commanded him not to have any private meetings; because it was against his law, and he was ordained of God, he should not have any.

Bunyan replied that Paul owned the powers that were in his day to be of God; yet he was often in prison under them for all that. " The law hath provided two ways of obeying; the one to do that which I, in my conscience, do believe that I am bound to do, actively; and where I cannot obey actively, there I am willing to lie down, and to suffer what they shall do unto me."

The position was very clearly stated and recognised by Bunyan, and there is no need to condemn either side. The prohibition of private meetings was a necessary and reasonable precaution at a time when the country had recently passed through a complete change of constitution following a long and bitter civil war; to have allowed these meetings would have been to encourage anarchy. Such general regulations are bound to weigh heavily on the conscientious objector. Bunyan realised that in general the law was reasonable, but he believed that the will of God at this point crossed the law of England. He was given every chance of submitting to the law, at his arrest, his trial, and afterwards in prison; and Cobb, if he was speaking with any authority, went a long way to meet Bunyan's scruples. But Bunyan steadily refused to make any compromise which might seem to weaken his faith in the eyes of his converts.

Meanwhile the coronation of King Charles had been fixed for the 23rd of April, and, as was customary, a number of prisoners were released. Bunyan had hoped to share in this general amnesty, but was told that as a convicted person he must sue out a pardon.

The midsummer assizes were held that year in August, and Bunyan made another effort to be freed, through his wife, who presented three separate petitions. She had already been up to London, and there had spoken with Lord Barkwood at the House of Lords, to whom she delivered a petition, which he took and presented to others of the Lords. They told her that they could not release him, but had committed his release to the judges at the next assizes. She now presented herself to the judges, and especially addressed herself to Judge Hale.

He treated her with sympathy, and she told him that she had four children that could not help themselves, and one of them blind, with nothing to live upon but the charity of others. " Hast thou four children ? " he asked ; " thou art but a young woman to have four children."

" My lord," she answered, " I am but mother-in-law to them, having not been married to him yet two full years. Indeed, I was with child when my husband was first apprehended, but being young and unaccustomed to such things, I being 'smayed at the news, fell into labour, and continued for eight

76

days, and then was delivered, but my child died."

After further talk Judge Hale said he could do nothing for her. Three courses were possible : either to apply to the King, or to sue out a pardon, or to get a writ of error ; the last was cheapest.

After this assize Bunyan was allowed a good deal of liberty by the jailer. He resumed his preaching, exhorting the people of God to be steadfast and to have nothing to do with the Common Prayer Book. On the 28th of September a church meeting was held, the first recorded in the *Church Book* since January, at which it was agreed that as " certaine of our friendes have not onely withdrawne themselves but also otherwaies failed, some of our friends be sent to admonish them of the same " [1] ; amongst them Brother Bunyan was to go to Brother Robert Nelson and Sister Manly. He is mentioned again at the next meeting held on the 26th of October.

He even was allowed to go to London, which made his enemies so angry that they accused him of plotting to raise an insurrection, and threatened to dismiss and indict the jailer. Thereafter his " liberty was more straitened than it was before ; so that I must not look out of the door."

Bunyan's name does not reappear in the *Church Book* for several years. The record is carried on until March 1663 ; after which there is a gap for four and a half years.

[1] *Church Book*, f. 25.

JOHN BUNYAN

The following February (1662) Bunyan expected to have been brought up at the sessions and " very soundly dealt withal " ; but he was passed over. In April, when the assizes were again held at Bedford, he asked the jailer to put his name among the felons, and extracted a promise from the judge and the high sheriff that he should appear at the assizes. The justices and the clerk of the peace, however, so arranged matters that he was again passed over, the clerk of the peace even going so far as to erase his name from the calendar prepared for the judge. So once more Bunyan was disappointed of liberty.

Meanwhile, though prevented from preaching, Bunyan was reaching a larger public by writing, and shortly afterwards he published *I will pray with the Spirit and with the understanding also, or a Discourse concerning Prayer*, a treatise which reflects his sense of resentment at his continued captivity and his indignation against the new Book of Common Prayer ; it is probably founded on his sermons preached when he was at liberty in the autumn of the year before.

Prayer, to be real, must be spontaneous and from the heart, overwhelmed by its sense of the danger of sin or by a sweet sense of mercies received. Thus Jacob, David, Daniel and others prayed, " not by fits and starts, nor yet in a foolish, frothy way, to babble over a few words written in a paper," but mightily, fervently, and continually. The communion and solace with Christ, when the affections
78

are indeed engaged in prayer, is so great that the saints will lose their lives rather than forgo the blessing.

All this [he continues] is too, too evident by the ignorance, profaneness, and spirit of envy, that reign in the hearts of those men that are so hot for the forms, and not the power of praying. Scarce one of forty among them know what it is to be born again, to have communion with the Father through the Son ; to feel the power of grace sanctifying their hearts : but for all their prayers they still live cursed, drunken, whorish, and abominable lives, full of malice, envy, deceit, persecuting of the dear children of God. O what a dreadful after-clap is coming upon them ! which all their hypocritical assembling themselves together, with all their prayers, shall never be able to help them against, or shelter them from.[1]

Prayer was difficult enough for the true Christian ; even Paul said, " We know not what we should pray for as we ought." The apostles themselves, when they were at the best, when the Holy Ghost assisted, could only express themselves with sighs and groans.

But here now, the wise men of our days are so well skilled as that they have both the manner and matter of their prayers at their finger-ends ; setting such a prayer for such a day, and that twenty years before it comes. One for Christmas, another for

[1] *Works*, i, 625.

79

Easter, and six days after that. They have also bounded how many syllables must be said in every one of them at their public exercises. For each saint's day also, they have them ready for the generations yet unborn to say. They can tell you also when you shall kneel, when you shall stand, when you should abide in your seats, when you should go up into the chancel, and what you should do when you come there.[1]

One word spoken in faith (and Bunyan emphasises it with a finger pointing in the margin) is better than a thousand prayers, as men call them, written and read, in a formal, cold, lukewarm way.

Then he turns contemptuously to consider some of the views of his opponents :

" Give me leave a little to reason with thee, thou poor, blind, ignorant sot." How can they pray " Our Father " when the devil is their father, causing them to persecute the true children of God ? But prayer is not merely from the mouth ; the best prayers have often more groans than words ; and those but a lean and shallow representation of the heart, life, and spirit of the prayer. David, with the pains of hell catching hold on him, needed no bishop in a surplice to learn him to say " O Lord, I beseech thee, deliver my soul."

There are, however, certain arguments in favour of forms of prayer which Bunyan will at least answer ;

[1] *Works*, i, 628.

such, for instance, as the problem of teaching children to pray. Even so he will have none of it ; to teach children forms of prayer is the next way to make them cursed hypocrites and to puff them up in pride. The way men learn to pray is by conviction for sin ; and so should children. Let them be told of their wretched state and condition ; of hell-fire and their sins, of damnation and salvation ; " this will make tears run down your sweet babes' eyes and hearty groans flow from their hearts."

Bunyan ends with a word of reproof for those who hinder praying with the spirit. They openly blaspheme the Holy Ghost ; they commit the cursed abomination of Jeroboam in preventing the people from coming to Jerusalem to pray. They advance the form of their own or others' inventing before the Spirit of prayer which is God's special and gracious appointing.

The Lord in mercy [he ends] turn the hearts of the people to seek more after the Spirit of prayer ; and in the strength of that, to pour out their souls before the Lord. Only let me say it is a sad sign, that that which is one of the most eminent parts of the pretended worship of God is Antichristian, when it hath nothing but the tradition of men, and the strength of persecution, to uphold or plead for it.[1]

In the summer of 1663 Bunyan evidently thought

---

[1] *Ibid.,* p. 640.

that he was about to die, for at the end of the first edition of *Christian Behaviour* he added the note :

Thus have I in a few words written to you before I die, a word to provoke you to faith and holiness, because I desire that you may have the life that is laid up for all men that believe in the Lord Jesus, and love one another when I am deceased. . . . Farewell, From my place of confinement in Bedford this 17th of the 4th month [July] 1663.

It is not clear from these words whether he was ill or whether he was expecting to die on the scaffold.

Christian Behaviour is thus a kind of testament, and is concerned with the practical duty of Christians in their personal relationships as husband, wife, child, master, servant, or neighbour ; and it has this special interest, that it can be compared with similar works by other religious writers, especially Fuller and Jeremy Taylor in the seventeenth century.

After some preliminary considerations on Faith and Works, Bunyan begins with the head of the family. He is to labour to bring his family to public worship, and if they will not come, then to bring godly men to them. He must not neglect reading the Word and prayer, nor must he allow ungodly, profane, or heretical books or discourse ; though in indifferent matters Christians must have their liberty, those which strike at faith or holiness must be abandoned. As for outward things, he must take care that his children have a convenient livelihood, but at the same time not to grasp the world in his heart or his coffers.

The husband, if his wife is a believer, should so love her that their life together may preach the carriage of Christ to his Church. If she be an unbeliever, then he has a double duty towards her. He must act according to his principles, labouring to overcome her evil and frowardness with patience and meekness ; taking fit opportunities to convince her, but speaking to the purpose, for it is no matter for many words, but pertinent ; and all should be done without rancour.

The instructions for parents are admirable. He urges them to take heed of filling their children's heads with whimsies and unprofitable notions ; gentleness and patience must be used in instruction ; they must be convinced that the things taught are not fables, but realities. As for correction, fair words should be used to win them from evil, and those sober, few, and pertinent, adding always some suitable sentence of the Scripture. Rude and ungodly companions must be avoided ; their naughtiness should be disliked soberly ; " let all this be mixed with such love, pity, and compunction of spirit, that if possible they may be convinced you dislike not their persons, but their sins. This is God's way." [1]

[1] *Works*, ii, 559.

With the next two injunctions, however, modern psychologists would heartily disagree :

(5) Be often endeavouring to fasten on their consciences the day of their death, and judgment to come. Thus also God deals with his (Deut. xxxii. 29).

(6) If thou art driven to the rod, then strike advisedly in cool blood, and soberly show them, (1) their fault ; (2) how much it is against thy heart thus to deal with them ; (3) and that what thou dost, thou dost in conscience to God, and love to their souls ; (4) and tell them, that if fair means would have done, none of this severity should have been. This, I have proved it, will be a means to afflict their hearts as well as their bodies ; and it being the way that God deals with his, it is the most likely to accomplish its end.

Finally, certain cautions must be particularly observed :

1. Take heed that the misdeeds for which thou correctest thy children be not learned them by thee. Many children learn that wickedness of their parents for which they beat and chastise them.

2. Take heed thou smile not upon them, to encourage them in small faults, lest that thy carriage to them be an encouragement to them to commit greater.

3. Take heed thou use not unsavoury and unseemly words in thy chastising of them, as railing, miscalling, and the like : this is devilish.

4. Take heed thou do not use them to many chiding words and threatenings, mixed with lightness and laughter; this will harden. Speak not much, nor often, but pertinent to them with all gravity.[1]

In theory Bunyan held the most horrible views about children, but in practice he was humaner than his doctrine; for Charles Doe noted, with a hint of disapproval, that he was an indulgent father almost to a fault.

About the duties of a master Bunyan's remarks are uncompromising. He must be careful not to cheat his servants either by understating the work or by " wire-drawing " them to such wages as are too little for the labour to be performed. Nor must he make a gain of his religion by underpaying the servants because of their religious privileges. " I have heard some poor servants say that in some carnal families they have had more fairness of dealing than among professors. This stinketh."

A wife is to be subject to her husband, and to do all as having her warrant, licence, and authority from him; nor must she ever offer to overtop her husband; but she is not to be her husband's slave; she is his yoke-fellow, his flesh and his bones. The wife is master next her husband, and is to rule in his absence; and even in his presence she is to guide the house, and to bring up the children, pro-

[1] *Works*, ii, 559.

vided she do it as the adversary have no occasion to speak reproachfully.

As for children, they are bound by the law of God and nature to obey their parents. In general they should always count their parents better than themselves, neither despising nor having slighting thoughts about them ; nor arguing that because " my father is now poor, and I am rich, and it will be a disparagement or at least a hindrance to me to show that respect to him as otherwise I might "—this is to argue like an atheist and a beast. A child is a debtor to his parents for three reasons : for his being in the world, for their care taken of him when he was helpless, for the pains taken to bring him up, and, Bunyan adds feelingly, " until thou hast children of thine own, thou wilt not be sensible of the pains, watchings, fears, sorrow, and affliction that they have gone under to bring thee up."

If the parents be godly, what must their sufferings be when they see their children going astray, every miscarriage going to the heart for fear God should take occasion thereat to shut them up in hardness for ever ? If however the children are godly and the parents wicked, then—

Let thy bowels yearn towards them ; it is thy parents that are going to hell !

As I said before to the wife, touching her unbelieving husband, so now I say to thee. Take heed of a parroting tongue ; speak to them wisely, meekly, and humbly ; do for them faithfully without repining ; and bear, with all child-like modesty, their reproaches, their railing, and evil speaking. Watch fit opportunities to lay their condition before them. O ! how happy a thing would it be, if God should use a child to beget his father to the faith ! Then indeed might the father say, With the fruit of my own bowels hath God converted my soul. The Lord, if it be his will, convert our poor parents, that they, with us, may be the children of God.[1]

From duties in the home Bunyan passes to the Christian's duty in the world, laying heavy stress on the practical side of faith, and dealing with the sins especially rife among professors—covetousness, pride, and uncleanness. Covetousness, or evil desire, is the first mover, and gives to every sin its call both to move and to act ; it encourages the seller to magnify the value of his goods and the buyer to depreciate them ; it persuades men to be mean in their charity, and to repent of their generosity ; it is the sin of idolatry.

Pride is of two kinds : of the heart, and outward pride. Pride of the heart takes reproof for sin unkindly, and worse from a poor saint than a great doctor ; outward pride " is discovered by mincing words, a made carriage, and an affecting the toys and baubles that Satan and every light-hearted fool bringeth into the world. Adultery, or uncleanness,

[1] *Works*, ii, 564.

is akin to these sins ; it shows itself in three ways : a wanton eye, immodest talk, and light and wanton apparel.

The attire of an harlot is too frequently in our day the attire of professors ; a vile thing, and argueth much wantonness and vileness of affections. If those that give way to a wanton eye, wanton words, and immodest apparel, be not whores, &c., in their hearts, I know not what to say. Doth a wanton eye argue shamefacedness ? Doth wanton talk argue chastity ? And doth immodest apparel, with stretched-out necks, naked breasts, a made speech, and mincing gaits, &c., argue mortification of lusts ? If any say, that these things may argue pride as well as carnal lusts ; well, but why are they proud ? Is it not to trick up the body ? And why do they with pride trick up the body, if it be not to provoke both themselves and others to lusts ? God knoweth their hearts without their outsides : and we know their hearts by their outsides.[1]

The book concludes with a number of general reasons and exhortations to good works.

Christian Behaviour shows Bunyan at his best, applying his faith to the practical problems of life with a deal of wisdom and common sense. There is no compromise where principles are concerned, and Bunyan's lack of scholastic training is here an advantage to him because he is not distressed by

[1] *Works*, ii, 569.

fine shades of difference ; a thing is either good or bad. But his faith at this time, though rigid and defined by hard outlines, is not wanting either in insight or sympathy. He realises, for instance, how difficult it is for a Christian wife, married to a godless husband, to treat him with the respect which her duty demands. Much of the value of the book comes from his own experiences as child, as husband, and as parent, for in practical things as well as in spiritual problems he observed himself, analysing his own experiences and comparing them with what he had observed in others.

While in prison Bunyan also tried his hand at verses, but without much success. These were afterwards brought together in a volume entitled *One thing is needful,* and include meditations upon death, judgment, heaven and hell, and *Prison Medita-tions,* addressed to a friend who had sent him con-solation. They are written in a tinkling " eight and six," scarcely a suitable medium for Bunyan's message ; even Heaven becomes a plaster affair in such a metre :

> If all that build, do build to suit
>   The glory of their state,
> What orator, though most acute,
>   Can fully heaven relate ?
>
> If palaces that princes build,
>   Which yet are made of clay,
> Do so amaze when much beheld,
>   Of heaven what shall we say ?

> It is the high and holy place ;
>   No moth can there annoy,
> Nor make to fade that goodly grace
>   That saints shall there enjoy.[1]

There are nearly three hundred verses of the same poetic standard.

But, though later he succeeded in writing better verse, Bunyan was no poet, and when he fettered himself with rhyme his pen could only turn off jingling platitudes, as in *Prison Meditations*, whose complacent sentiments were far from what he was actually feeling :

> The prison very sweet to me
>   Hath been since I came here,
> And so would also hanging be,
>   If God would there appear.
>
> Here dwells good conscience, also peace,
>   Here be my garments white ;
> Here, though in bonds, I have release
>   From guilt, which else would bite.
>
> When they do talk of banishment,
>   Of death or such-like things ;
> Then to me God sends heart's content,
>   That like a fountain springs.[2]

What he really felt at this time is expressed in *Grace Abounding*:

When I at first began to think of this [that he would be hanged] it was a great trouble to

---

[1] *Works*, iii, 730.   [2] *Ibid.*, i, 64.

me : for I thought with myself, that in the condition I now was in, I was not fit to die, neither
indeed did think I could if I should be called
to it. Besides, I thought with myself, if I should
make a scrambling shift to clamber up the ladder,
yet I should either with quaking or other symptoms
of fainting, give occasion to the enemy to reproach
the Way of God and his people, for their timorous-
ness. This therefore lay with great trouble upon
me, for methought I was ashamed to die with a
pale face, and tottering knees, for such a cause as
this.

In *Ebal and Gerizim*, the other verse piece, he tried
the rhymed decasyllabic couplet, but hardly in the
manner of Mr. Waller's refined numbers.

> Besides what I said of the Four Last Things,
> And of the weal and woe that from them springs ;
> An after-word still runneth in my mind,
> Which I shall here expose unto that wind
> That may it blow into that very hand
> That needs it.   Also that it may be scann'd
> With greatest soberness, shall be my prayer,
> As well as diligence and godly care ;
> So to present it unto public view,
> That only truth and peace may thence ensue.[1]

In *The Holy City, or The New Jerusalem*, published
in 1665, Bunyan wrote in a new vein. The book
originated, so he explains in the epistle to four
sorts of readers, upon a certain first day when the
brethren with him in prison were expecting that

[1] *Ibid.*, iii, 737.

something should be spoken out of the Word for their mutual edification. It was Bunyan's turn to speak, but he found himself empty, spiritless, and barren until he cast his eye upon the description of the New Jerusalem in the 21st chapter of Revelation :

Upon which when I had considered a while, methought I perceived something of that jasper in whose light you there find this holy city is said to come or descend ; wherefore having got in my eye some dim glimmerings thereof, and finding also in my heart a desire to see farther thereinto, I with a few groans did carry my meditations to the Lord Jesus for a blessing, which he did forthwith grant according to his grace ; and helping me to set before my brethren, we did all eat, and were well refreshed ; and behold also, that while I was in the distributing of it, it so increased in my hand, that of the fragments that we left, after we had well dined, I gathered up this basketful. Methought the more I cast mine eye upon the whole discourse, the more I saw lie in it. Wherefore setting myself to a more narrow search, through frequent prayer to God, what first with doing, and then with undoing, and after that with doing again, I thus did finish it.[1]

In the discourse he quotes first the whole text (Revelation xxi. 10–27, xxii. 1–4), and then taking it phrase by phrase, he treats the narrative as allegory and so expounds it at considerable length. Thus,

[1] *Works*, iii, 397.

on the sentence " And the street of the city was
pure gold, as it were transparent glass," he asks
four questions : What the street is ? Why not streets
but street ? Why called pure gold ? Why it should
look like transparent glass ? The exposition of the
first point begins thus :

A street ordinarily is the place of common concourse, and the place of continual open salutation,
and taking acquaintance one of another ; and as
touching this street, we are also to understand it of
the open and common place or way of God's worship,
in which saints salute each other and acquaint themselves together ; also here the world are converted,
saints built up and edified, &c. " Wisdom crieth
without ; she uttereth her voice in the streets,"
saith Solomon ; " she crieth in the chief place of
concourse, in the openings of the gates ; in the city
she uttereth her words " (Prov. i. 20, 21). That is,
in the public and righteous ordinances of the Lord
Jesus, which he hath ordained in his church, for
men to travel and trade in, for the good and whole-
some merchandise of heaven, as the men of this
world do for the things thereof in the streets and
open places of their cities and places of privilege
(Prov. viii. 1–3 ; ix. 1–3).[1]

Compared with some of the books which Bunyan
had written in prison *The Holy City* is formal, passion-
less, and somewhat laboured, though the interpretation is certainly edifying and quite devoid of

[1] *Ibid.*, p. 436.

the rhapsodies which the Revelation evokes in some enthusiasts. It has, however, this importance in the development of Bunyan's mind, that he is here decoding an allegory, and so insensibly preparing his mind for reversing the process in *Pilgrim's Progress.*

In 1666 was printed *Grace Abounding.* The change of tone between the preface to this book and that in *The Holy City* is very marked. In *The Holy City* he begins apologetically; the men of this world will laugh that one so poor and inconsiderable as himself should venture on the exposition of a hard and knotty Scripture. In *Grace Abounding* he writes as a leader of the saints with the authority of an apostle:

Children, Grace be with you, Amen. I being taken from you in presence and so tied up that I cannot perform that duty from God doth lie upon me to you-ward, for your further edifying and building up in faith and Holiness, &c. yet that you may see my soul hath fatherly care and desire after your spiritual and everlasting welfare, I now once again, as before from the top of Shenir and Hermon, so now from the lions' dens, from the mountains of the leopards do look yet after you all, greatly longing to see your safe arrival into THE desired haven.

He is no longer a brother, but the father of those whom he has begotten to faith. Now he sends them this discourse that they may remember their own
94

experience of grace, and the Word which gives them hope :

If you have sinned against the Light, if you are tempted to blaspheme, if you are down in despair, if you think God fights against you, or if heaven is hid from your eyes ; remember it was thus with your father ; *but out of them all the Lord delivered me.*

Something clearly had happened in Bunyan's life which had not only given him immense self-confidence but had entirely changed his relations with the rest of the congregation at Bedford. Unfortunately, there is a complete gap in the records of Bunyan's life for these years ; no entries were made in the *Church Book* between 1663 and 1668, and Bunyan wrote, or at least published, nothing further until 1671. At this time of persecution several of the congregation deserted and conformed, and it may be that Bunyan in his period of liberty in 1666 had rallied the survivors and reunited them before he was sent back to prison. The tone of the preface seems to suggest that he and his " dear children " had recently shared some deep and very moving experience ; if so, the preface to *Grace Abounding* was probably written at the beginning of his second imprisonment, or shortly before it.

Grace Abounding is neither a diary nor a scientific record, but a work of art ; and in his desire to give God the glory he suppressed or minimised much that he had received from man and woman. It is clear, for instance, that he owed his conversion, in the first place, to his first wife and the parson of Elstow ; but he says little of them. Except that his wife was threatened with a miscarriage he says nothing of the births of his children, events usually of some significance in the life of a man. He omits to mention the death of his first wife or his marriage with his second. Even in the material circumstances that he records there is distortion and exaggeration ; he over-emphasises the poverty of his father and the insufficiency of his own education. But then *Grace Abounding* is not a piece of spontaneous autobiography ; after the first edition was published he went over it and made considerable and significant additions which not a little improve the artistic effect of the whole ; such, for instance, as the account of his escapes from drowning, or the occasion when his substitute was shot during the Civil War.

Bunyan felt himself to be a man marked out for distinction, one specially chosen by God, and he was not a little proud of being the hero of so desperate a struggle with the Tempter ; hence he tends to intensify the light and the shadow to gain a striking effect. He is no ordinary sinner, but the chief of sinners, whose conversion was the more miraculous ; besides, like Paul on the road to Damascus, he had heard the very voice of God, and at other times the voice of Satan too. The message of the book is that if the chief of sinners could become the leader of the saints, then smaller men with lesser temptations might take infinite hope from the titanic struggles of their spiritual father. It would be unjust to call Bunyan spiritually arrogant, but in writing *Grace Abounding* he was, like Milton, not ignorant of his parts.

To the saints of Bunyan's persuasion *Grace Abounding* is a rare illustration of a Christian soul called by God ; but the worldly-minded see in it a considerable work of art, akin to the great spiritual autobiographies in the English language, and not the least of those books which have led men to be absorbed in the workings of the human mind. But, for anyone who does not belong to Bunyan's little flock, it is a little surprising that he should have overlooked the fourth Gospel in his reading. To the text "God is love" he joined "whom the Lord loveth he chasteneth," and, "if ye be without chastisement, whereof all are partakers, then are ye bastards, and not sons."

It was the custom in Bunyan's church for the new convert to make a public declaration of the workings of grace in his soul ; *Grace Abounding* is thus Bunyan's thesis for the spiritual doctorate.

G

THE PASTOR

CHAPTER III

THE PASTOR

DURING the second imprisonment (1666–72) Bunyan published little, and then only at the end of the period; but he was allowed considerable liberty and busily occupied. In October 1668 the records in the *Church Book* begin again, and Bunyan is often mentioned as taking a leading part in the affairs of his church. Persecution was slackening off, and the faithful brethren once more began to take steps to restore discipline. There is a very different temper in the entries in the book, and as events showed the moving spirit in the church was Brother Bunyan.

On the 30th of November the entry reads:

Many of the friends having in these troublous times withdrawne themselves from close walking with the church, and not being reclaimed by those admonitions, that as time would serve, had been sent to them formerly, some also being guilty of more grosse miscarriages, the Congregation having kept certaine dayes wth fasting and prayer bewailed their fall, did now agree in a solemne way to renew their admonitions.[1]

Accordingly Brothers Samuel and John Fenn and Brother Bunyan are to admonish Robert Nelson for his withdrawing from the church and other mis-

[1] *Church Book*, f. 27.

carriages; Brother Samuel Fenn and Brother John Croker are to go to Brother Richard Dean and rebuke him; Brother Bunyan and Brother Harrington are to send for Brother Merrill and admonish him concerning his withdrawing from the church and his conformity to the world's way of worship; Brother Bunyan and Brother Cooper are to admonish Brother Coventon and endeavour his conviction for his sin in withdrawing from the church assemblies.

The sequel, however, is missing, as nothing further is recorded until 10th September 1669, except for a brief entry on the 14th of June; possibly Brother Bunyan had returned to jail for a space.

In September, however, the reforms were continued with renewed zeal. Brother Coventon and Brother Wallis having utterly neglected the office of deacon, were judged unworthy of that honourable employment and divested of all authority. On the 14th of October Brother Man and Brother Croker delivered their reports on the erring brethren, Merrill, Dean, and Coventon.

As for bro. Merrill though their words, and carriage were so winning, and full of bowells, that he could not well break out into that impatiency as he had sometimes done; yet after some windings he began in an obscure way to charge the Church, with rebellion, and also with taking some portions of Scripture that made for their purpose, and refusing the other. To which things though he was fully answered; yet to their last entreating of him to come before the Church, he peremptorily with great confidence replyed That he knew them well enough already and would have no more to do with them; bidding them do their worst, saying Their faire speeches should not flatter him, &c.[1]

A month later Brother Wallis was reported to be promising reformation. On the 16th of December Brother Coventon was reported to be hopefully recovering from his backsliding. Brother Bunyan and Brother Breeden were to go to Humphrey Merrill, and Brother Bunyan and Brother Whiteman to Richard Dean. On the 14th January 1670 it was agreed that Humphrey Merrill, unless he should repent in the meanwhile, should be cut off. Brother Bunyan and Brother Man were to reason with Mr. Sewster about his desire of breaking bread with the congregation without sitting down with them as a member, and Brother Samuel Fenn and Brother Bunyan to discourse with Sister Landy about her scruples.

A full assembly of the congregation was held a week later and Humphrey Merrill solemnly cast out of the church for—

1. Breaking Covenant with God, and fellowship with this Congregation.

2. ffor an open recanting his profession at a general quarter sessions.

[1] *Church Book*, f. 28.

3. And rejecting and trampling upon the admonitions, and intreaties, and all indeavours of the
Church to recover him to amendment of life : dis-
dainefully returning, for their care, and indeavours
to reclaime him, such ungodly railings as these :
That they had their hands in the blood of the King :
That they were disobedient to government : And
that they were not a church ; despising also the Gifts
of, and doctrines of God in, the Congregation :
together with severall other false, and heinous
accusations.[1]

The decision was testified by seven brethren,
Bunyan signing fourth. At the same time nine
new brethren from Gamlingay were admitted.

During these months there had been difficulties
with Brother Whitbread, who absented himself
from a meeting on 21st February 1669 and was
admonished accordingly in a long but friendly
epistle. His reply was read on the 25th of March,
but being found unsatisfactory a further epistle was
sent, pointing out more severely that he had neglected
the assemblies of the congregation, casting off the
care of the church in general and of its members in
particular ; he had also neglected the Lord's Table,
fasting, and prayer in the church ; and all this for
the space of seven years.

The second answer was read on the 14th of April.
Brother Whitbread defended himself and expressed

---

[1] *Church Book*, f. 29.

his dissatisfaction with some of the practices of the church ; nevertheless he would not justify himself. " I have had, and yet remaine under, burthens and troubles, you have not bene acquainted with. I am conscious to my self, of my owne inclinations, and overmuch prepenseness to dejectedness : if you observe not in me the egressions of sorrow, as you have seen in others acknowledgements ; I desire you to believe my experience of deceit in such things : and concernements to avoide such impressions, are the causes of it." [1] Brother Whitbread, in fact, " who was once a fair and flourishing professor," was at this time in the iron cage of despair.

The correspondence dragged on for another two and a half years. In February 1670 the brethren were seriously disturbed " concerning his con-formity to y⁰ nationall worship," and later they were threatening withdrawal. Finally he submitted, and on 9th November 1671 was received back again into full communion. The controversy takes up a considerable space in the *Church Book*, and was evidently a matter of great consequence to the con-gregation at Bedford ; socially Brother Whitbread was one of their most important brethren.

There were other defaulters. On the 25th of Feb-ruary Brother Samuel Fenn and Brother Bunyan reported their conversations with Sister Landy and were also instructed to inform adjacent congregations

[1] *Ibid.*, f. 49.

of their proceedings against Merrill. Three months later Brother John Fenn certified that he and Brother Bunyan " had indeavoured to speake wth Richard Deane, but (he continually indeavouring to avoide their delivering their message by keeping out of the way) they could by no means accomplish it, whereupon the Church did agree shortly to proceed further with him." [1] At the next meeting, held on the 8th of June, Brother Samuel Fenn and Brother Bunyan were instructed to have further discourse with Sister Landy.

Meanwhile there were other troubles without.[2]

On Lords-day (*May* 15) at the dwelling-house of one *John Fen*, a Haberdasher of Hatts, many persons being assembled for Religious Exercise ; One *West* and *Feckman* (two Apparitors) by a Warrant from one Mr. *Foster*, who is a Justice of Peace, and the Commissaries Deputy, did enter the House, and force the Meeters to Mr. *Fosters* House, who fined every one of them severally, according to their reputed abilities ; and committed the Preacher to Prison, for words he spake against the Church of *England*, then occasioned by the discourse of Mr. *Foster*.

---

[1] *Church Book*, f. 36.

[2] The details which follow are taken from an anonymous pamphlet, " A true and impartial *narrative* of some *Illegal* and *Arbitrary* proceedings by certain Justices of the Peace and others, against several innocent and peaceable *Nonconformists* in and near the Town of *Bedford*, upon pretence of putting into execution the late Act against *Conventicles*," 1670. I have quoted rather fully because of the detailed picture which the pamphlet gives of Bunyan's fellow worshippers.

106

THE PASTOR

The business of distraining was in the charge of Thomas Battison, one of the Bedford churchwardens, who, collecting the overseers of the poor and the constables, began with John Bardolf, a maltster.

Whilst *Battison* and the Officers were debating in the open Yard before the Malthouse Door, a great number of all sorts of persons were gathered about them, expressing (by turns) their indignation against him, for attempting this against *Bardolf*; whom the whole Town knew to be a just and harmless man ; and the common sort of the people covertly fixing a Calves tayl to *Battisons* back, and deriding him with shouts and hollows, he departed without taking any distress there.

Next Battison went to Edward Coventon's house whence he removed a brass kettle.

When he had brought it to the street-door, none of the Officers would carry it away ; neither could he hire any to do it in two hours time, though he offered money to such needy persons among the company as wanted bread ; At last he got a youth for sixpence to carry the Kettle less way than a stones-throw, to an Inn-yard where before he had hired a Room to lodge such goods, under pretence to lodge Grain : but when the Youth had carried the Kettle to the Inn-gate, (being hooted at all the way by the common Spectators) the Inn-keeper would not suffer the Kettle to be brought into his Yard ; and so his man set it in the middle of the street, None regarding it, till towards night a poor woman that receiveth alms was caused by an Overseer to carry it away.

After this unfortunate beginning the work of distraining went on more smoothly. The following week Mr. Foster himself led the party. They began with Nicholas Hawkins, a cutler, who was fined 40*s.*, but as his goods had been removed and there was smallpox in the house the officers refused to enter. Thence they passed to Michael Shepheard, a shoemaker, fined 5*s.* and 12*d.* more for not answering a question. Thomas Honeylove was next visited, but as there was smallpox there too, the party proceeded to Thomas Cooper, a heelmaker, from whom they took the wood especially cut for his trade. Thence to John Crocker, dealer in linen drapery, who had already been put into custody for refusing to help the officers. His fine was £3, but he had removed his shop goods, and so Battison passed on to Daniel Rich, a tanner, and constable of his ward. He was fined 5*s.* for his wife, and his best coat was distrained; thence to John Spencer, a grocer, fined 40*s.*, and William Jay, a baker, fined 5*s.* ; and so to his next-door neighbour, Edward Isaac, blacksmith, fined 40*s.* for himself and his wife. From him they took away locks, shovels, and his anvil; " and *Battison* would have pulled down the Forge-Bellows also, but it required more time and labour, than his itch to greater prizes in other places would allow him."

Then they went on to Thomas Arthur, pipe maker, whose fine was £6. As his door was locked an attempt was made to force it, but it was opened from inside.

Mr. *Foster* enters, and distreyning all the Goods within doors and without, the said *Arthur* desired to know, how much Money had distreyned for ? to whom the said Mr. *Foster* replied, that they distreyned for eleven pounds ; thereupon *Thomas Arthur* desired to see the Warrant : which being produced, he seeing himself therein but six pound, told Mr. *Foster* so : to which Mr. *Foster* answered, *that there was five pound more for keeping his Door locked.* When *Thomas Arthur* perceived that Mr. *Foster* would distreyn all his Goods ; he said, *Sir, What shall my Children do, shall they starve ?* Mr. Foster replied, *that so long as he was a Rebel, his Children should starve.*

This incident is but a specimen of what went on in Bedford when a dissenter hunt was in progress. On this occasion the sufferers were popular ; at other times the " common spectators " hooted the victims. In the circumstances it was not unnatural for Bunyan's fellow saints to have sought consolation in the doctrine that God's mercy in another world was to be confined solely to those whom he had specially called by his grace.

In the following April (1671) Robert Nelson and Richard Dean were cut off from and cast out of the congregation. Brother Whiteman and Brother Neh. Coxe were appointed to declare the just and fearful sentence that in the name and power of the Lord Jesus had been denounced against Dean. Robert Nelson's case needed further consideration because he could not, for the present, be spoken with. It was also agreed that this Epistle should be sent to the neighbouring churches :

Dearly beloved breth:

Grace be with you by Jesus Christ your Lord and oures. Amen.

Blessed be God, and the ffather of our Lord Jesus Christ, for the grace bestowed upon you, brethren, and for the faith you have in the Lord Jesus, and your love to all the saintes.

We, your brethren, the Congregation of Christ in and about Bedford, give you to understand w^t troubles have come upon us, by reason of Robert Nelson and Richard Deane, persons sometimes members of this congregation, but now cut off and cast out from the Church of God for these wickednesses following

Things laide to ye charge of Richard Deane

1. ffor that he after a very ungodly manner separated himself from this congregation, and the word, and ordinances of Christ therein.

2. He after this lived a loose and ungodly life accompanyed with defrauding in his Calling ; selling to severall persons deceitfull goodes, to the great scandall of our profession.

3. ffor speaking contemptuously of the Church.

THE PASTOR

4. He went in the name of the Church, and yet wholly without their knowledge or consent, to beg the charity of yᵉ good people of St. Neots ; ffor all which things, and many others he hath bene admonished, by the space of some years ; yet could not be brought to repentance for the same.

Robert Nelson's practises were as followeth.

He forsooke the Church with the order of the Gospell therein.

2. In a great assembly of the Church of England, he was openly and profanely bishopt, after the Antichristian order of that Generation ; to yᵉ great profanation of God's order and heartbreaking of his Christian brethren.

ffor these he hath bene often admonished, and that for the space of sixe or seven yeares, but hath Contemned and slighted the same. And besides he hath so trampled upon our holy order and fellowship, that for the space of eight or nine yeares, he could not be gotten to be present, at any of our Church Assemblyes.

Wherefore we warne and beseech you in the name of our Lord Jesus Christ, that as occasion or opportunity offereth it self, you carry it towards them in all things, as becometh a people that keep faithfull with the Lord.

Written by the appointment of the congregation, and on their behalf signed by

SAM: FFENNE.   JOH: WHITEMAN.
JOH: BUNYAN: JOH: FFENNE.[1]

[1] *Church Book*, f. 45.

Meanwhile Bunyan was still nominally a prisoner, and possibly to justify himself in the eyes of the world he wrote and published his next book, *A Confession of Faith and Reason of my Practice* (1672). In this book he defines his position towards those with whom he differs, both the " outwardly profane " and those " visible saints " that differ about water baptism ; but he was mainly concerned with stating his own creed as clearly as he could. There is not much that he had not said before, but now it was arranged in orderly paragraphs, each article being justified by the scriptural authority on which it was based. Anyone who is interested in the doctrinal differences between Bunyan and the Church of England can find it most easily summarised in this book.

He restates the old question of the law and grace thus :

I believe, therefore, that the righteousness, and redemption, by which we that believe, stand just before God, as saved from the curse of the law, is the righteousness, and redemption, that consists in the personal acts and performances of this child Jesus ; this God-man the Lord's Christ : it consisteth, I say, in his personal fulfilling the law for us, to the utmost requirement of the justice of God.[1]

As regards justification, election, and calling, Bunyan's doctrine was hardening into a rigid form

[1] *Works*, ii, 595.

of predestination. Being sinful creatures, nothing done by men can procure of God the imputation of the righteousness of Christ. Justification from the curse of the law is wrapt up in the personal doings and sufferings of Christ; faith in that, and that only, can justify a sinner in the sight of God. This faith is not to be found with any but those in whom the Spirit of God by mighty power works it, and is effectually wrought in none but those which before the creation of the world were appointed unto glory.

Election is free and permanent, being founded in grace and the unchangeable will of God; it was before the foundation of the world, and so before the elect themselves had being in themselves. " The decree of election is, so far off from making works in us unseen, the ground or cause of the choice : that it containeth in the bowels of it, not only the persons but the graces that accompany their salvation. And hence it is that it is said we are predestined ' to be conformed to the image of his son ' (Rom. viii. 29), not because we are, but that we SHOULD be holy and without blame before him in love (Eph. i. 4)." Election does not forestall or prevent the means which are of God appointed to bring men to Christ, but rather puts a necessity upon their use and effect.

To effectual calling, the Holy Ghost must accompany the word of the gospel. Its signs are great

H   113 awakenings about the world to come, and the glory of unseen things, the resurrection of the dead and eternal judgment ; the salvation which God has prepared for them that love him.

He adds that all the Holy Scriptures are the words of God, and of themselves, without the addition of human inventions, are able to make the man of God perfect in all things. God committed the Scriptures to writing that we might be instructed to Christ, taught how to believe, how to understand what is sin, and how to avoid its commission. Jesus Christ by the word of the Scriptures will judge all men at the day of doom.

Magistracy is God's ordinance ; and " many are the mercies we receive by a well qualified magistrate, and if any shall at any time be otherwise inclined, let us show our Christianity in a patient suffering for well doing, what it shall please God to inflict." This paragraph, which concludes the confession of faith, seems to have been inserted as a reminder that Bunyan is by his principles no law-breaker.

Bunyan passes thence to the reasons of his practice in worship. In holy things the Christian is not to have communion with those that profess not faith and holiness, because the church must dwell by herself and not be unequally yoked with unbelievers. In civil matters, however, he is not altogether cut off from the profane.

He reverently esteems the two ordinances of

Christ, water baptism and the supper of the Lord, but does not regard them as fundamentals. A visible saint is so made by grace but not by baptism; "for he must be a visible saint before, else he ought not to be baptized."

Take it again: "Baptism makes thee no member of the Church, neither particular nor universal; neither doth it make thee a visible saint; it therefore gives thee neither right nor being of membership at all." Later he says that a failure in such a circumstance as water doth not unchristianise us. "Neither if I be baptized am I the better, neither if I be not, am I the worse before men." Nevertheless, a year after writing this book Bunyan took his own infant son to the parish church to be baptized.

The office of pastor had been vacant for some time during the persecutions and the question of appointing a successor arose. On 24th November 1671 it is noted that "The Church was also minded to seeke God about the choyce of bro. Bunyan to the office of an elder that their way in that respect may be cleared up to them." [1]

The proposal was confirmed on the 31st of December, and a general meeting appointed for 21st January 1672 for solemn ratification.

After much seeking God by prayer, and sober conference formerly had, the Congregation did at

[1] *Church Book*, f. 49.

this meeting with joynt consent (signifyed by solemne lifting up of their hands) call forth and appoint our bro: John Bunyan to the pastorall office, or eldership: And he accepting thereof, gave up himself to serve Christ, and his church in that charge ; and received of the elders the right hand of fellowship.

The same time also, the Congregation having had long experience of the faithfulnes of bro: Joh: ffenne in his care for the poor, did after the same manner solemnely choose him to the honourable office of a deacon, and committed their poor, and purse to him ; and he accepted thereof, and gave up himself to ye Lord and them in that service. . . .

The Congregation did also determine to keep the 26th of this instant as a day of fasting and prayer, both here, and at hanes, and at Gamlinghay, solemnely to recommend to the grace of God bro: Bunyan, bro: ffenne, and the rest of the brethren ; and to intreat his gracious assistance and presence with them in their respective worke whereunto he hath called them.[1]

On 15th March 1672 King Charles issued the Declaration of Indulgence, and on the 8th of May a petition was presented by John Fenn, John Bunyan, and other prisoners in Bedford jail. Meanwhile Bunyan had applied for recognition as a preacher, and the next day he was formally licensed " to bee a Teacher of the Congregation allowed by Us in the

[1] *Church Book*, ff. 50, 51.

House of Josias Roughed, Bedford, for the use of such as doe not conforme to the Church of England, who are of the Perswasion commonly called Congregationall. With further licence and permission to him the said John Bunyan to teach in any other place licensed by Us according to our said Declaration." [1]

The petition for release was referred to the sheriff of the county, who certified that the prisoners were detained for nonconformity ; and on the 17th of May by order in Council their petition was forwarded to the Attorney-General that the names of the prisoners might be inserted in the General Pardon. This pardon was not formally sealed until the 13th of September, though there is little doubt that Bunyan was at liberty.

The first years of Bunyan's pastorate were not very happy ; and the entries made by his own hand in the *Church Book* suggest that all was not well with the congregation at Bedford. The 14th July 1673 was to be " kept as day of humiliation and praire upon several waighty accounts." Four months later (18th of November) " was cast out of the church the wife of our Bro. Witt, for railling, and other wicked practises. Concluded that som dayes be sett appart for humiliation with fasting and prayer to god because of som disorders amongst som in the congregation specialy for that som have run in to

1 Brown, p. 215.

debt more then they can satisfie, to the great dishoner of god and scandall of religion." [1]

On 10th May 1674 a church meeting was holden at Bedford " to pray to god to bless admonition upon four in the congregation that had transgressed : at the same meeting was our sister Elizabeth Bigbie openly rebuked for an immodest lieing in a chamber several nights with wherein also lay a young man no body being in the house but them two. At the same meeting also, the Church was told that our Sister Landy had bin admonished for withdrawing communion againe, for countenancing Card-play, and for deceiving the Church with her former seeming repentance. At the same meeting our sister Abiss did declare her repentance for her former withdrawing from the congregation, to their good satisfaction and was received in againe. At the same meeting the Church was told that our Sister Elizabeth Maxey had bin admonished for disobedience to her parents, to witt, for calling her father lier, and for wicked carriages to her mother." [2]

But worse than these was an unfortunate scandal in which Bunyan had been unwittingly involved a few weeks before. One of his flock was a certain Agnes Beaumont, a young woman of twenty-two, who has left an account of a most distressing experience which she suffered in 1674 because of her devotion to Bunyan's ministrations. She was a

[1] *Church Book,* f. 54. [2] *Ibid.,* f. 54.

most zealous follower, and had been one of his first converts after he had been appointed to the pastorate. But at this time her father disapproved of her going to the meetings because of some rumours about Bunyan then current. Her story, as she tells it, is a remarkably vivid piece of introspective prose writing, and gives a clear picture of Bunyan as he appeared to an admiring disciple.[1]

In February the weather was very cold and severe, so that it was impossible for her to walk through the snow from Edworth, where she lived, to the meeting at Gamlingay. Nor could she find anyone to give her a ride :

O, thought I, that God would please to put it in the heart of somebody to come this way and carry me, and make some way or other for my going. Well, still I waited with my heart full of fears lest I should not go. At last unexpected came Mr. Bunyan, and called at my brother's house as he went to the meeting, but the sight of him caused sorrow and joy in me ; I was glad to see him but I was afraid he would not carry me to the meeting behind him, and how to ask him I did not know for fear he

[1] The manuscript is in the British Museum (Egerton, 2414). The story was printed several times in the eighteenth century, with other accounts of religious experience. In 1801 it was published separately as a twopenny tract with the title *Real Religion : exemplified in the singular experiences and great suffering of Mrs. Agnes Beaumont.* In the printed version, however, Agnes's vivid narrative has been somewhat watered down. I have ventured to modernise spelling and punctuation.

should deny me. So I got my brother to ask him. So my brother said to him, " I desire you to carry my sister today behind you."

And he answered my brother very roughly and said, " No, not I, I will not carry her."

Those was cutting words to me indeed which made me weep bitterly. My brother said to him again, " If you do not carry her, you will break her heart."

And he replied with the same words again that he would not carry me. And he said to me, " If I should carry you, your father would be grievous angry with me."

Said I, " If you please to carry me I will venture that."

So with a great many intreaties at last my brother did prevail with him, and I did get up behind him ; but oh how glad was I that I was going ! But I had been but just on horseback, as I heard afterwards, but my father came to my brother's, to some of the men that was at work and asked them who his daughter rode behind. They answered such an one ; with that my father fell into a passion and ran down to the close end, thinking to have met me in the fields where he intended to have pulled me off of the horse back, he was so angry because some had incensed him against Mr. Bunyan. But we was gone by first ; but to speak the truth I had not gone far, behind him, but my heart was puffed up with pride and I began to have high thoughts of myself and proud to think I should ride behind such a man as he was ; and I was pleased that anybody did look after me as I rode along. And sometimes he would be speaking to me about the things of God, as we went along. And indeed I thought myself a happy body that day ; first that it did so please God to make way for my going to the meeting, and then that I should have the honour to ride behind him. But as you will understand, my pride had a fall.

Bunyan was unable to give her a ride back and when at last she reached home that night she found her father in bed and the door shut against her so that she was compelled to spend the night in the barn. Next morning he remained obdurate and refused to have anything to do with her, even threatening to cut her out of his will, unless she promised not to go to Bunyan's meetings again without his leave ; after a deal of heart-searching, she agreed and they were reconciled. This was on the Monday morning. On Tuesday night the father suddenly died, with no one in the house but Agnes. The funeral was fixed for the Thursday, but an amiable neighbour raised the report that Agnes had poisoned her father and that Bunyan had supplied the poison. An inquest was held and Agnes triumphantly acquitted of all scandal.

Meanwhile other tales were set going. A clergyman reported at Baldock Fair that Bunyan and Agnes Beaumont had been criminally conversant. Another version was that Bunyan was a widower and had persuaded Agnes to poison her father, so that they might marry.

There is nothing in the narrative to suggest that there was the slightest truth in all this tattle, though possibly Agnes Beaumont's devotion to her pastor was a little indiscreet; but it is not surprising that Bunyan's writings at this time should have reflected some of the bitterness which he was feeling. His next works were *Reprobation Asserted*, *Light for them that sit in darkness*, and *Instruction for the Ignorant*.

Bunyan and his religion at its worst is shown in *Reprobation Asserted*, a piece of cold-hearted casuistry, inspired partly by religious hate.

The argument, which is aridly logical, may be summarised briefly. God, from the beginning of the world, has chosen and foreappointed certain individuals to be his elect; others he has not chosen; these are reprobate. In this he acts as the potter, choosing one piece of clay to be made into a vessel of honour, another into a vessel of dishonour. "Reprobation is before the person cometh into the world, or hath done good or evil."[1] This is clear from Paul's words to the Ephesians: "God hath chosen us in Christ before the foundation of the world." If the elect are so forechosen, reprobation also follows, "it being the negative of electing love; that is, because God elected but some, therefore he

[1] *Works*, ii, 338.

left the rest ; these rest, therefore, must needs be of as ancient standing under reprobation as the chosen under election." So punctual, exact, and to a tittle is this decree of election that God has not only confined the number and quantity of the persons but also determined and measured, and that before the world, the number of the gifts and graces that are to be bestowed on these members in general ; and also what graces and gifts are to be bestowed on this or that member in particular.

Accordingly ignorant men much quarrel at eternal reprobation, " concluding for want of knowledge in the mystery of God's will that if he reprobate any from eternity, he had as good have said, ' I will make this man to damn him ; I will decree this man, without any consideration, to the everlasting pains of hell.' " But, says Bunyan, for God to reprobate and to appoint to eternal condemnation are two distinct things. He expresses this even more clearly in the form of an *Objection* :

From what hath been said, there is concluded this at least, That God hath infallibly determined, and that before the world, the infallible damnation of some of his creatures : for if God hath before the world [was made] bound some over to eternal punishment, and that as you say, for sin ; then this determination must either be fallible or infallible ; not fallible, for then your other position of the certainty of the number of God's elect, is shaken unless you hold that there may be a number that shall neither go to heaven nor hell. Well then, if God hath indeed determined, fore-determined, that some must infallibly perish; doth not this his determination lay a necessity on the reprobate to sin, that he may be damned; for, no sin, no damnation; that is your own argument.[1]

No, answers Bunyan, a man is not necessarily bound to sin, even if God has not chosen him to be one of his elect and foreknows that he will sin.

But, says the objector, God has already determined that this creature shall be damned; does it not follow he must sin of necessity, seeing that, according to the argument, he cannot be damned without sinning?

Not at all, answers Bunyan.

Nor have those who are foreordained to eternal reprobation any quarrel with God; for God to elect is an act of sovereign grace; for him to pass by or refuse to elect is an act of sovereign power, not of injustice. God, however, does not refuse his gospel to be preached to sinners; he commands it.

But is it possible that the tender of grace, made in the gospel and " thus offered to the reprobate, should by him be thus received and embraced, and he live thereby? "

Certainly not, answers Bunyan, for election comes

[1] *Works*, ii, 342.

from God, and man can do nothing by himself to gain it.

The point is exceedingly subtle; and it comes to the same conclusion, for the reprobate is pitched into hell-fire either way.

> Thus you see again [Bunyan concludes] that the non-elect perish by reason of sin, notwithstanding present mercy, because of eternal justice; and that the elect are preserved from death, though they sin and are obnoxious to the strokes of present justice, by reason of eternal mercy. What shall we say then? Is there unrighteousness with God? God forbid: "He hath mercy on whom he will have mercy, and compassion on whom he will have compassion" (Rom. ix. 15).[1]

After all, Bunyan had endured much for his principles.

It is only fair to add that Dr. John Brown rejected *Reprobation Asserted* from the Bunyan canon, mostly on points of style.[2] But the same hard, logical style is to be found in *Questions about the nature and perpetuity of the Seventh-day Sabbath*, wherein Bunyan was again arguing a point of doctrine. The arguments for reprobation and election arise quite naturally from Bunyan's doctrine of grace. Others of his disciples have felt no difficulty about the book; Doe included it in the list of Bunyan's works, though not

---

[1] *Ibid.*, ii, 358.   [2] Brown, p. 228.

in his folio, and Offor, who was the first to reprint it, calls down the Divine Blessing on his " attempt to spread this important, although to many, unpalatable doctrine."

The only consoling thought about the terrible doctrine of predestination is that few hold it until convinced that they are themselves on the short list for appointment to heaven. When a sensitive man, such as William Cowper, is persuaded to believe it without self-assurance, he is likely to go mad.

In *Light for them that sit in Darkness* (1675) Bunyan for the first time considers Jesus Christ at length, and his thesis is to demonstrate how Jesus set himself to save sinners and how he accomplishes it. In the opening sections the book is very closely written, being a logical demonstration based on the Bible, with each argument and position stated or demonstrated under various heads, but as it continues a note of ecstasy appears which had not been heard in Bunyan's writings for a long time. He begins with the promises of a Saviour, thence to the birth of Christ, to demonstrate that he was indeed man. It was necessary for him to become man if he was to be also a Saviour.

God could not communicate himself to us, nor take us into the enjoyment of himself, but with respect to that flesh which his Son took of the Virgin, because sin stood betwixt. Now this flesh only was the holy lump, in this flesh God could dwell ; and forasmuch

as this flesh is the same with ours, and was taken up
with intent that what was done in and by that, should
be communicated to all the children; therefore
through that doth God communicate of himself
unto his people—" God was in Christ, reconciling
the world unto himself" (2 Cor. v. 19). And " I
am the way," saith Christ; " no man cometh unto
the Father but by me " (Jno. xiv. 6).[1]

Being man, Jesus was subject to the law and its
penalties. He was not himself a sinner, by his own
acts or doings; but God charged him with our sins
and he paid the penalty accordingly by undergoing
the wrath of God. Yet his punishment could not be
everlasting, for punishment is everlasting because the
sinner can never repay the debt due to God for his
sins. Christ had in himself the perfection of all
graces and virtues; his rising from the dead the
third day did not invalidate his sufferings, but showed
the power of his merit.

This doctrine is proved by nine demonstrations,
and its application is that it shows the wisdom of
God in devising means to reconcile sinners to himself,
being thereby a just God and yet a saviour—by
" just," as usual, Bunyan meaning one who punishes,
not one who spares. His justice is seen in that he
respected not persons, but condemned even his Son.
Above all it shows God's love and mercy.

Another use of the doctrine is that it gives men

[1] *Works,* i, 405–6.

the best discovery of God and of himself. The doctrine of Christ crucified cries aloud to sinners that sin has made their condition terrible, for sin is so dreadful a thing as to break the heart even of the Son of God; how then shall a poor, wretched, impenitent, damned sinner wrestle with the wrath of God? Nor can his good deeds help him; for by this doctrine—Christ died for our sins—God damns to death and hell the righteousness of the world. Christ must die, or man be damned.

The doctrine also furnishes argument to withstand the temptations of the devil. When the soul is earnestly looking to Jesus Christ three things usually afflict it : dreadful accusations from Satan; grievous defiling and infectious thoughts; a strange readiness in our nature to fall in with both; so that the, soul struggles very grievously.

The fly in the spider's web is an emblem of the soul in such a condition—the fly is entangled in the web; at this the spider shows himself; if the fly stir again, down comes the spider to her, and claps a foot upon her; if yet the fly makes a noise, then with poisoned mouth the spider lays hold upon her; if the fly struggle still, then he poisons her more and more. What shall the fly do now? Why, she dies, if somebody does not quickly release her. This is the case of the tempted; they are entangled in the web, their feet and wings are entangled; now Satan shows himself; if the soul now struggleth, Satan laboureth to hold it down ; if it now shall make a noise, then he bites with blasphemous mouth, more poisonous than the gall of a serpent ; if it struggle again, then he poisoneth more and more, insomuch that it needs, at last, must die in the net, if the man, the Lord Jesus, help not out.[1]

Finally, Christ is thus made very precious to believers, rejoicing in his love.

Light for them that sit in Darkness was followed by *Instructions for the Ignorant*, written in the form of a catechism, question and answer, intended for children and the simple-minded of all ages. It is, in fact, an example of the kind of religious training for the young which Bunyan had advocated in *Christian Behaviour* twelve years before.

Opening with the nature of God and the devil, he passes thence to death eternal and the original sin of Adam, whereby all his descendants come into the world polluted by his sin. Thence *Question* and *Answer* pass to this terrible dialogue :

QUESTION. But do not some hold that we are sinners only by imitation ?

ANSWER. Yes, being themselves deceived. But God's word saith, we are children of wrath by nature, that is, by birth and generation.

QUESTION. Can you bring further proof of this ?

ANSWER. Yes : in that day that we were born, we were polluted in our own blood, and cast out

---

[1] *Works*, i, 435.

to the loathing of our persons. Again, the children of old that were dedicated unto the Lord, a sacrifice was offered for them at a month old, which was before they were sinners by imitation (Ezek. xvi. 4-9 ; Num. xviii. 14-16).

QUESTION. Can you make this appear by experience ?

ANSWER. Yes : the first things that bloom and put forth themselves in children, shew their ignorance of God, their disobedience to parents, and their innate enmity to holiness of life ; their inclinations naturally run to vanity. Besides little children die, but that they could not, were they not of God counted sinners ; for death is the wages of sin (Rom. vi. 23).

QUESTION. What is sin ?

ANSWER. It is transgression of the law (1 Jno. iii. 4).[1]

And so backwards and forwards over sin, confession of sin, damnation, faith, prayer, to the final unamiable reflection—" Consider how sweet the thought of salvation will be to thee when thou seest thyself in heaven, whilst others are roaring in hell."

Though the first years of his pastorate at Bedford were full of troubles, elsewhere Bunyan had his consolations. After his release from prison " he preached the gospel publicly at Bedford, and about the counties, and at London, with very great success, being mightily followed elsewhere." [2]

[1] *Works*, ii, 677.   [2] Doe, in *Works*, iii, 766.

This success was more than compensation for the difficulties at home; it is reflected in Bunyan's next book, *The Strait Gate* (published in 1676), which is written in a new and happy mood.

The text was taken from Luke xiii. 24 : " Strive to enter in at the strait gate ; for many, I say unto you, will seek to enter in, and shall not be able." He was addressing " professors," having been persuaded more than ever by the experiences of these last months that God had chosen him as one of his apostles. As his hearers were as familiar as he was with the Scriptures there was no need to prove doctrinal points. Instead he spoke from his own experiences, and especially from those which he had gained during the last seven years as he went round with his brethren to collect the stray sheep.

The Strait Gate marks a third stage in the development of Bunyan's mind. The first was in the early days when, as a convert full of ecstasy, he had tried to frighten his hearers away from the edge of hell-pit ; the second was the period of bitterness and aridity when the enthusiasm had died down, and he had taken refuge in a logic based on Scripture. Now both ecstasy and logic were succeeded by a wise humanity. The change of mood led to a change of style. Instead of stringing texts together under headings, he quotes much less and relies more on his own words and the illustrations which he drew from his ample converse with saints and sinners of many kinds. Bunyan is always at his best when speaking of his human experiences, with the result that *The Strait Gate* is full of those touches of homely example and striking phrases which make Bunyan so eminently readable to those who have no sympathy with his religious beliefs.

The sermon is cut on the usual pattern, but it contains such gems as these :

This word lies in the Bible as excellent salves lie in some men's houses, thrust into a hole, and not thought on for many months, because the household people have no wounds nor sores. In time of sickness, what so set by as the doctor's glasses and gally-pots full of his excellent things ? but when the person is grown well, the rest is thrown to the dunghill.[1]

The world will seek to keep thee out of heaven with mocks, flouts, taunts, threatenings, jails, gibbets, halters, burnings, and a thousand deaths ; therefore strive ! Again, if it cannot overcome thee with these, it will flatter, promise, allure, entice, entreat, and use a thousand tricks on this hand to destroy thee ; and observe many that have been stout against the threats of the world, have yet been overcome with the bewitching flatteries of the same.[2]

Religious duties are not the only striving times ; he that thinks so is out.[3]

How few among the many, yea, among the swarms of professors, have heart to make conscience of

[1] *Works*, i, 364.   [2] P. 370.   [3] P. 370.

walking before God in this world, and to study his glory among the children of men! How few, I say, have his name lie nearer their hearts than their own carnal concerns! Nay, do not many make his Word, and his name, and his ways, a stalking-horse to their own worldly advantages ? [1]

It is common with a professing people, when they hear a smart and a thundering sermon, to say, Now has the preacher paid off the drunkard, the swearer, the liar, the covetous, and adulterer ; forgetting that these sins may be committed in a spiritual and mystical way. [2]

" I say unto you ! " Had not the Lord Jesus designed by these words to show what an overthrow will one day be made among professors, he needed not to have *you'd* it at this rate, as in the text, and afterwards, he has done ; the sentence had run intelligible enough without it ; I say, without his saying " I say unto you." [3]

The person whose words we have now under consideration was no blundering raw-headed preacher, but the very wisdom of God, his Son, and him that hath lain in his bosom from everlasting, and consequently had the most perfect knowledge of his Father's will, and how it would fare with professors at the end of this world. [4]

At this day, those things that now these " many " count sound and good, will then shake like a quagmire, even all their naked knowledge, their feigned faith,

[1] P. 373.   [2] P. 373.   [3] P. 373.   [4] P. 374.

pretended love, glorious shows of gravity in the face, their holiday words and specious carriages, will stand them in little stead. I call them holiday ones, for I perceive that some professors do with religion just as people do with their best apparel—hang it against the wall all the week, and put it on on Sundays. For as some scarce ever put on a suit but when they go to a fair or a market, so little house religion will do with some : they save religion till they go to a meeting, or till they meet with a godly chapman.[1]

It is the devil and sin that carry away the cart-loads, while Christ and his ministers come after a gleaning.[2]

In almost every house, you may find brass, and iron, and lead ; and in every place you may find hypocritical professors, but the saved are not these common things ; they are God's peculiar treasure.[3]

Among the multitude of them that shall be damned, professors will make a considerable party.[4]

Some bad fishes, nay, I doubt a great many, will be found in the net of the gospel at the day of judgment. Watch and be sober, professors." [5]

The dog doth not loath that which troubleth his stomach because it is there, but because it troubleth him ; when it has done troubling of him, he can turn to it again, and lick it up as before it troubled him.[6]

[1] *Works,* i. 377.   [2] P. 380.   [3] P. 382.
[4] P. 381.   [5] P. 383.   [6] P. 384.

THE PASTOR

There will be many a one, that were gallant professors in this world, be wanting among the saved in the day of Christ's coming; yea, many whose damnation was never dreamed of. Which of the twelve ever thought that Judas would have proved a devil ? [1]

Such poor sinners are much like to the wanton boy that stands at the maid's elbow, to blow out her candle as fast as she lights it at the fire. [2]

Those touches are to be met with in the earlier works, but neither so many nor so good. At the same time *The Strait Gate*, and especially *The Pilgrim's Progress*, and *Mr. Badman*, give the impression that Bunyan has been reading books which were not intended for edification. Towards the end of *The Strait Gate* he gives the characters of twelve kinds of professors, such as the " temporising latitudinarian."

He is a man that hath no God but his belly, nor any religion but that by which his belly is worshipped. His religion is always, like the times, turning this way and that way, like the cock on the steeple ; neither hath he any conscience but a benumbed and seared one, and is next door to a downright atheist ; and also is one of the many that " will seek to enter in, and shall not be able." [3]

Or the double-faced professor :

And he is for God and for Baal too ; he can

be anything for any company; he can throw stones with both hands; his religion alters as fast as his company; he is a frog of Egypt, and can live in the water and out of the water; he can live in religious company, and again as well out. Nothing that is disorderly comes amiss to him; he will hold with the hare, and run with the hound; he carries fire in the one hand, and water in the other; he is a very anything but what he should be. This is also one of the many that " will seek to enter in, and shall not be able." [1]

It is clear that Bunyan had been reading one of the many books of " Characters " which were so popular in the seventeenth century, for the style and turn of phrase are too closely modelled to be coincidence. The type can be illustrated from Bishop Earle's description of " A Church Papist."

A CHURCH PAPIST is one that parts his religion betwixt his conscience and his purse, and comes to church not to serve God but the king. The face of the law makes him wear the mask of the gospel, which he uses not as a means to save his soul, but charges. He loves Popery well, but is loath to lose by it; and though he be somewhat scared with the bulls of Rome, yet they are far off, and he is struck with more terror at the apparitor. Once a month he presents himself at the church, to keep off the church-warden, and brings in his body to

[1] *Works,* i, 389.

save his bail. He kneels with the congregation, but prays by himself, and asks God forgiveness for coming thither. If he be forced to stay out a sermon, he pulls his hat over his eyes, and frowns out the hour ; and when he comes home, thinks to make amends for this fault by abusing the preacher. . . .

In 1675 the Declaration of Indulgence was withdrawn, persecution of the dissenters was renewed, and for about six months Bunyan was again a prisoner.

To distract his thoughts he set to work on his next book, *The Pilgrim's Progress.*

THE WRITER

CHAPTER IV

THE WRITER

BUNYAN wrote *The Pilgrim's Progress* when he was forty-eight; it was his twenty-fourth publication. His mind had mellowed very quickly since his election to the pastorate; and now he gathered up all the experiences of the last twenty-five years into the book which is among the dozen greatest in the English language.

The idea came to him in 1676. He was finishing off *The Strait Gate* in prison, and had fallen into the allegorising vein when he found that a new and very abundant spring had been tapped. The parables he had interpreted often enough; and in earlier years his mind had constantly dramatised a mental conflict. Hitherto, however, he had not attempted anything very elaborate in this kind, but as he began to turn some of his experiences with professors into a parable, his whole life seemed to burgeon out into a continuous story: it was already written in his mind, and

> Still as I pulled, it came.

So at vacant times he wrote, at first with no intention to do more than divert his mind; but the story grew to an end, and, after some discussion, he decided to print it. It was published in 1678, and immediately

141

a second edition was demanded, to which several important additions were made.

The Pilgrim's Progress is another version of the spiritual life and adventures of John Bunyan. It is the story of *Grace Abounding* rewritten in a new form ten years afterwards.

It has its literary ancestors, but there is no need to look too closely for an immediate model. The adventurous journey was old when the *Odyssey* was written ; and it has the great advantage as a form that the beginning and the ending are quite natural. The idea, too, of man's life as a pilgrimage had been popular since the Middle Ages ; and for generations the virtues and vices had been personified. Bunyan, in fact, borrowed his form from the common stock of story-tellers ; for his teaching he used the dialogue, so common in the sixteenth and seventeenth centuries as the vehicle for the theological or social argument ; for his story he owed something to romances of the kind beloved by Beaumont's citizen-grocer.

The origins of the incidents are mainly threefold. Much was taken from books, of which naturally the Bible contributed most, though a good deal came from secular and less edifying works, the fight with Apollyon or the escape from Doubting Castle, for instance. Some episodes are deliberate allegorising, elaborately compounded for edification, such as the Interpreter's House or Despair's vision, for which no less than seventeen texts are quoted as sources. But

the best are derived from personal reminiscences
recorded with but slight alteration.

There are three principal methods of creating an
allegorical character. The first is to take a virtue,
or quality, or the like, describe its characteristics,
and personify it with a name, as Spenser personifies
Fear :

> All arm'd from top to toe,
> Yet thought himself not safe enough thereby
> But fear'd each shadow moving to and fro,
> And his own arms when glittering he did spy,
> Or clashing heard, he fast away did fly,
> As ashes pale of hue, and wingy heeled ;
> And evermore on danger fix'd his eye,
> 'Gainst whom he always bent a brazen shield,
> Which his right hand unarmèd fearfully did wield.[1]

A few of Bunyan's characters are similarly compounded, such as Pope and Pagan ; the former—

Though he be yet alive, he is, by reason of age,
and also of the many shrewd brushes that he met
with in his younger days, grown so crazy and stiff
in his joints, that he can now do little more than
sit in his cave's mouth, grinning at pilgrims as they
go by, and biting his nails because he cannot come
at them.[2]

The second method is to describe minutely a
living man who is a notable example of some particular
"humour" or vice ; this was Ben Jonson's manner.

---

[1] *Fairy Queen*, III, xii, 12.   [2] *Works*, iii, 116.

The greatest artists combine the two in creating a type which is compounded partly of a real original, partly from imagination. This was Shakespeare's method, and for the most part Bunyan's. The best characters in *The Pilgrim's Progress* had their living models, and some of them can be plausibly identified in the *Church Book*. Christian is Bunyan himself; Evangelist, who meets him at the beginning of his journey, is John Gifford; Prudence, Piety, and Charity had perhaps some resemblance to the poor women of Bedford. Christian's companions, Faithful and Hopeful, conversed with the false professors on their way as Brother Bunyan and Brother Samuel Fenn, or John Fenn or Brother Whiteman, had conversed with Friend Talkative, or By-ends or Save-all, Money-love or Ignorance, when sent forth by the congregation at Bedford.

It is not unlikely also that some particular traits of Robert Nelson or Richard Dean are to be found in the description of the reprobates who infested the path of the Pilgrim. So with the conversations; Mr. Worldly-wiseman's advice to Christian is very similar to the proposal which Mr. Cobb the clerk of the peace had made to Bunyan in Bedford jail.

With the other great books which are sometimes termed " universal " *The Pilgrim's Progress* appeals to different kinds of readers for entirely different reasons. The religious will regard it as an object-lesson, a guide-book to the Holy Land; that was

Bunyan's intention after—but not before—he had
finished writing. But the surprising fact is that
Bunyan, who had hitherto written as the zealous
teacher of a narrow puritan sect, should now produce
a book which has been accepted into the shelves
of Christian sects in a vast number of languages, for
even Catholics have adopted the book, after a few
necessary deletions. The explanation is given in
Bunyan's own account of its beginnings :

> I only thought to make
> I knew not what : nor did I undertake
> Thereby to please my neighbour ; no, not I ;
> I did it mine own self to gratify.

It was the first time in his life that he had ever allowed
himself to write a book for the sheer artistic joy of
creation ; and the writing of it gave him such pleasure
that, as a true Puritan, he felt a little ashamed of
the result, though fully conscious that it could
compare favourably with any piece of literature.

> Now my little book,
> (Though void of all those paintings that may make
> It with this or the other man to take),
> Is not without those things that do excel,
> What do in brave but empty notions dwell.

And as Bunyan has himself made this claim, it is not
unreasonable for the critic to disregard the message
of *The Pilgrim's Progress* and to discuss it as a work
of literature.

K   145

The first paragraph is a perfect opening, which excites the reader and compels his attention :

As I walked through the wilderness of this world, I lighted on a certain place, where was a den ; and I laid me down in that place to sleep ; and as I slept, I dreamed a dream. I dreamed, and, behold, I saw a man clothed with rags, standing in a certain place, with his face from his own house, a book in his hand, and a great burden upon his back. I looked and saw him open the book, and read therein ; and as he read, he wept and trembled ; and not being able longer to contain, he brake out with a lamentable cry, saying, " What shall I do ? "

It is often said that Bunyan owed his style to the Bible, and to a large extent this is true ; whole paragraphs in the *Progress* are composed of a mosaic of texts, and, even when he is not quoting, the rhythms of the Bible run constantly through his head :—

Now when he began to sweep, the dust began so abundantly to fly about, that Christian had almost therewith been choked. Then said the Interpreter to a damsel that stood by, " Bring hither the water, and sprinkle the room."

Yet the passages in the *Progress* which give most pleasure, at least to reprobate readers, are those which could not possibly be mistaken for quotation from the Scriptures :—

This town of Fairspeech, said Christian, I have

heard of ; and, as I remember, they say it is a wealthy place.

BY-ENDS. Yes, I will assure you that it is ; and I have very many rich kindred there.

CHRISTIAN. Pray, who are your kindred there, if a man may be so bold ?

BY-ENDS. Almost the whole town ; and in particular, my Lord Turn-about, my Lord Time-server, my Lord Fair-speech (from whose ancestors that town first took its name), also Mr. Smooth-man, Mr. Facing-both-ways, Mr. Any-thing, and the parson of our parish, Mr. Two-tongues, was my mother's own brother, by father's side ; and to tell you the truth, I am become a gentleman of good quality, yet my great-grandfather was but a waterman, looking one way and rowing another, and I got most of my estate by the same occupation.

CHRISTIAN. Are you a married man ?

BY-ENDS. Yes, and my wife is a very virtuous woman, the daughter of a virtuous woman ; she was my Lady Feigning's daughter, therefore she came of a very honourable family and is arrived to such a pitch of breeding, that she knows how to carry it to all, even to prince and peasant. It is true we somewhat differ in religion from those of the stricter sort, yet but in two small points ; first, we never strive against wind and tide ; secondly, we are always most zealous when religion goes in his silver slippers ; we love much to walk with him in the street, if the sun shines, and the people applaud him.[1]

It is this kind of writing, rather than the Biblical

[1] *Works*, iii, 132.

echoes, that makes the book; and the honest reader would probably confess that he found greater pleasure in the talk of By-ends and Mr. Moneylove than in the more edifying homiletics of Brother Hopeful; but then the Deadly Sins always were more interesting than the Cardinal Virtues, and so Bunyan found them. His saints, Christian, Hopeful, and Faithful are grave, austere men; they inspire great respect, but little love.

Of the elect Christian has most weaknesses, and therefore most humanity; he is somewhat easily led astray by Mr. Worldly-wiseman; he goes to sleep and loses his roll; he feels superior at outrunning Faithful, and immediately trips up; he leads Hopeful out of the way, he snubs him mercilessly and then leads him astray again; he is nearly drowned in the river at the very end of the journey. On the other hand, he has compensating virtues: he is always ready to acknowledge himself wrong; he goes back to fetch his roll; he fights valiantly against Apollyon; he manages the escape from Giant Despair's castle; and, in spite of all his temptations, he steadily plods through to the end. Yet for all his failings Christian remains an unsympathetic person; after his own lapses he has little justification for rounding so contemptuously on Ignorance, who really knew no better, or By-ends, who certainly meant well.

These pilgrims lack the virtues of the road; they are selfish. When Vain-confidence falls into the pit they call out to know what is the matter, but they only hear a groaning; it never occurs to them to lend a hand to fetch him out. Again, when Little-faith passes escorted by seven devils, they express sorrow and moralise over his fall at some length; they make no attempt to rescue him. Nor do they try to convince or convert the reprobates; Faithful complacently comments on Talkative, " But I am glad we had this little discourse with him; it may happen that he will think of it again; however, I have dealt plainly with him, and so am clear of his blood, if he perisheth." [1] But then God had not elected them; why should the saints trouble themselves over the predestinately damned?

It is perhaps unfair to analyse the characters and motives of the pilgrims too closely. *The Pilgrim's Progress* is not the story of the Christian faith, but of the puritan soul, and Puritanism was a faith which the individual found by himself.

There are noticeable changes of tone in the narrative which suggest that Bunyan sat down to his story in different moods, and it may be that the frequent formula, " Now I saw in my dream," marks the beginning of each day's work. For the most part allegory and narrative are one, but whenever a good incident occurs—such as the arrival at Vanity Fair, the fight with Apollyon, or the adventures in Giant Despair's castle—then the allegory is made to

[1] *Works*, iii, 125.

give place to the story. On the whole the style is level, but as the pilgrims enter the gate of the Holy City Bunyan pulls out all the stops into a grand harmony of triumph :

Now I saw in my dream that these two men went in at the gate ; and lo, as they entered, they were transfigured, and they had raiment put on that shone like gold. There were also that met them with harps and crowns, and gave them to them—the harps to praise withal, and the crowns in token of honour. Then I heard in my dream that all the bells in the City rang again for joy, and that it was said unto them, " ENTER YE INTO THE JOY OF YOUR LORD." I also heard the men themselves, that they sang with a loud voice, saying, " BLESSING, AND HONOUR, AND GLORY, AND POWER, BE UNTO HIM THAT SITTETH UPON THE THRONE, AND UNTO THE LAMB, FOR EVER AND EVER."

Now just as the gates were opened to let in the men, I looked in after them, and, behold, the City shone like the sun ; the streets also were paved with gold, and in them walked many men, with crowns on their heads, palms in their hands, and golden harps to sing praises withal.

There were also of them that had wings, and they answered one another without intermission, saying, " Holy, holy, holy is the Lord." And after that, they shut up the gates ; which, when I had seen, I wished myself among them.[1]

That is not quite the end of the story. Poor

[1] *Works,* iii, 166.

Ignorance finds his way across the river and knocks at the gate ; but his end is hell.

In 1678 Bunyan published a sermon on John vi. 37, " All that the Father giveth me shall come to me ; and him that cometh to me I will in no wise cast out." The discourse, which is entitled *Come and Welcome to Jesus Christ*, is addressed to the called sinner that is hesitating to answer, and it shows how fundamental was this doctrine of election in Bunyan's theological system, and with what casuistry he would defend it against an awkward text. The crux of the matter is in the word " all." Before enlarging on the message it was necessary to dispose of this difficulty.

This word all, therefore, must be limited and enlarged, as the truth and argument, for the sake of which it is used, will bear ; else we shall abuse Scripture, and readers, and ourselves, and all. " And I, if I be lifted up from the earth," said Christ, " will draw ALL men unto me " (Jno. xii. 32). Can any man imagine, that by ALL, in this place, he should mean all and every individual man in the world, and not rather that all that is consonant to the scope of the place ? And if, by being " lifted up from the earth," he means, as he should seem, his being taken up into heaven ; and if, by " drawing ALL men after him," he meant a drawing them unto that place of glory ; then must he mean by ALL men, those, and only those, that shall in truth be eternally saved from the wrath to come. " For God hath concluded them all in unbelief, that he might have mercy upon all " (Rom. xi. 32). Here again you have all and all, two alls; but yet a greater disparity between the all made mention of in the first place, and that all made mention of the second. Those intended in this text are the Jews, even all of them, by the first all that you find in the words. The second all doth also intend the same people; but yet only so many of them as God will have mercy upon. "He hath concluded them all in unbelief, that he might have mercy upon all." The all also in the text, is likewise to be limited and restrained to the saved, and to them only.[1]

He concludes the section with these words: "We must therefore diligently consult the meaning of the text by comparing it with other the sayings of God; so shall we be better able to find out the mind of the Lord, in the word which he has given us to know it by."[2] By such methods of argument it is possible to justify most doctrines.

After publishing *The Pilgrim's Progress* Bunyan set about a sequel, or rather a contrast, in *The Life and Death of Mr. Badman*, which came out in 1680. There is a contrast also in the method; instead of allegory, Bunyan writes a dialogue, with himself as Mr. Wiseman and his faithful disciple, Attentive, who discuss the lurid career of Mr. Badman, from birth to death, and take occasion by the way to enlarge on those sins which are most prevalent in

[1] *Works*, i, 242.   [2] *Ibid.*, i, 243.

Bedford, not least among the professors. At the same time Bunyan was conscious that his words reached a far wider circle than the church at Bedford; and he published this book to be read by the English people at large—

For that wickedness, like a flood, is like to drown our English world. It begins already to be above the tops of the mountains; it has almost swallowed up all; our youth, middle age, old age, and all, are almost carried away of this flood. O debauchery, debauchery, what hast thou done in England! Thou hast corrupted our young men, and hast made our old men beasts; thou hast deflowered our virgins, and hast made matrons bawds. Thou hast made our earth to reel to and fro like a drunkard; it is in danger to be removed like a cottage, yea, it is, because transgression is so heavy upon it, like to fall and rise no more (Isa. xxiv. 20). O! that I could mourn for England, and for the sins that are committed therein, even while I see that, without repentance, the men of God's wrath are about to deal with us, each having his slaughtering weapon in his hand (Ezek. ix. 1, 2). Well, I have written, and by God's assistance shall pray that this flood may abate in England; and could I but see the tops of the mountains above it, I should think that these waters were abating.[1]

Mr. Badman is the Puritan's answer to the rake, and

---

[1] *Ibid.*, iii, 592.

written in the form which he understood best, a realistic satire of manners.

Mr. Badman himself is a finely drawn character, and shows what Bunyan could have done had he cared to write pure fiction, for he is no painted vice but a very real person. He was bad from the first. " Sin, sin, and to do the thing that was naught, was that which he delighted in, and that from childhood." As a lad he was noted for his oaths; on which topic Mr. Wiseman could speak very feelingly, making clear distinctions between cursing and swearing. The kind of cursing that Badman used was that—

He would wish that evil might befall others; he would wish their necks broken, or that their brains were out, or that the pox or plague was upon them, and the like; all which is a devilish kind of cursing, and is become one of the common sins of our age. 2. He would also as often wish a curse to himself, saying, Would I might be hanged, or burned, or that the devil might fetch me, if it be not so, or the like. We count the Damn-me-blades to be great swearers, but when in their hellish fury they say, God damn me, God perish me, or the like, they rather curse than swear; yea, curse themselves, and that with a wish that damnation might light upon themselves; which wish and curse of theirs in a little time they will see accomplished upon them, even in hell fire, if they repent them not of their sins.

He would even curse his father's cattle.

He would wish their necks broke, their legs broke, their guts out, or that the devil might fetch them, or the like ; and no marvel, for he that is so hardy to wish damnation or other bad curses to himself, or dearest relations, will not stick to wish evil to the silly beast in his madness.[1]

When he grew up, Badman was put out as an apprentice to a good man, but he took no profit of his master, except to rob him. " Then he became a frequenter of taverns, and tippling houses, and would stay there until he was even as drunk as a beast." This form of sin was not uncommon in Bedford. During Bunyan's own ministry John Rush had been cast out " for being drunk after a very beastly and filthy manner, that is above the ordinary rate of drunkerds, for he could not be carried home from the Swan to his own house without the help of no less than three persons who, when they had brought him home, could not present him as one alive to his familie he was so dead drunke." [2]

After that he took up with loose women ; " and this roguery was his masterpiece, for he was a ring-leader to them all in the beastly sin of whoredom," on which subject Mr. Wiseman had a considerable repertory of anecdote, though a few moments before sternly he had condemned " beastly romances and books full of ribaldry, even such as immediately tended to set all fleshly lusts on fire." Herein he is

[1] *Works,* iii, 603.   [2] *Church Book,* f. 53.

true to life ; for the Puritan who will shrink from a bawdy tale as a snail from soot is usually well primed with a detailed store of notable examples of the wicked.

At length Badman set up in trade for himself with capital provided by his father, which however he soon spent on riotous living, and was obliged to look out for a rich wife. The account of his wooing is admirable ; the girl was godly, and Badman not a little diffident about his chances ; so he asked the advice of his companions.

Then one of them made reply, saying, " Since she is religious, you must pretend to be so likewise, and that for some time before you go to her. Mark therefore whither she goes daily to hear, and do you go thither also ; but there you must be sure to behave yourself soberly, and make as if you liked the Word wonderful well ; stand also where she may see you, and when you come home, be sure that you walk the street very soberly, and go within sight of her. This done for a while, then go to her, and first talk of how sorry you are for your sins, and show great love to the religion that she is of, still speaking well of her preachers and of her godly acquaintance, bewailing your hard hap that it was not your lot to be acquainted with her and her fellow-professors sooner ; and this is the way to get her. Also you must write down sermons, talk of scriptures, and protest that you came a-wooing to her, only because she is godly, and because you should count it your greatest happiness if you might but have such a one. As for her money, slight it, it will be never the
156

further off, that is the way to come soonest at it, for she will be jealous at first that you come for her money ; you know what she has, but make not a word about it. Do this, and you shall see if you do not entangle the lass." [1]

The plan succeeded ; to the terrible disillusionment of his wife. Next, having thrown off religion himself, he jeered at her devotions, and prevented her from going to sermons An actual case of this occurs in the *Church Book*, though six years after Bunyan's death, when " Alice Clark of Bedford was propounded and received into our fellowship both at the same meeting not as a president for others but because she feared she might be hindred her duty if her Husband heard it." [2]

When Mr. Badman had spent most of his wife's portion, he felt that if he was to maintain his trade and standing in the world, he would have to raise money by some fresh method. He therefore bought heavily and then declared a fraudulent bankruptcy by which he compounded with his creditors for five shillings in the pound, and so became possessed of their goods at a quarter of the value. This piece of dishonesty gives Mr. Wiseman his chance of discoursing at considerable length on the various dishonest practices of tradesmen, which were not unknown to the saints. Commercial dishonesty

[1] *Works*, iii, 618.   [2] *Church Book*, f. 85.

was heavily censured by Bunyan's congregation, when reported. In 1677, for instance, the congregation "withdrew Communyon from Edward Dent of Gamlingay, the matter of fact charged upon him was for being negligent and unfaithful as to the management of his sister's Imployment which he was intrusted with ; and alsoe for contracting many debts which he nether was able to pay, nether did he so honestlye and Christianly take care to pay his creditors in due time as he ought, though he had been often exhorted to it and admonished before by his brethren." [1]

There are other cases in the *Church Book* which show that Bunyan's detailed arraignment of these sins was particularly addressed to his own people as well as to the community in general. So much has Mr. Wiseman to say on the subject that Attentive ventures to remark, " Well, sir, now I have heard enough of Mr. Badman's naughtiness, pray now proceed to his death." To which Mr. Wiseman answers somewhat tartly, " Why, sir, the sun is not so low, we have yet three hours to night."

" Nay, I am not in any great haste, but I thought you had even now done with his life."

" Done ! " exclaims Mr. Wiseman, " no, I have

[1] *Church Book*, f. 66. When communion was " withdrawn " from a member he had either to satisfy the church by a repentance, which was no mere formula, or else he was " cast out " and excommunicated.

yet much more to say"; and with that launches out with a denunciation of the pride of Mr. Badman, which also is reflected in the unseemly carriages of some professors, particularly the women. "For my own part, I have seen many myself, and those church members too, so decked and bedaubed with their fangles and toys, and that when they have been at the solemn appointments of God in the way of his worship, that I have wondered with what face such painted persons could sit in the place where they were without swooning."[1] For example, "I once talked with a maid by way of reproof for her fond and gaudy garment. But she told me, the tailor would make it so; when alas! poor proud girl, she gave order to the tailor so to make it."

He concludes by saying, "I wonder what it was that of old was called the attire of a harlot; certainly it could not be more bewitching and tempting than are the garments of many professors this day."

Attentive is so much impressed by this remark that he wishes all the proud dames in England that profess were within the reach and sound of Mr. Wiseman's words; to which Mr. Wiseman replies, "What I have said I believe is true; but as for the proud dames in England that profess, they have Moses and the prophets, and if they will not hear them, how then can we hope that they should

[1] *Works*, iii, 644.

receive good by such a dull-sounding ram's-horn as
I am ? " [1]

The story of Mr. Badman is continued. He gets
drunk and breaks his leg. He falls dangerously sick,
and mightily penitent, if only God will grant him
a little longer life ; he becomes reconciled to his
wife ; " now she was his good wife, his godly wife,
his honest wife, his duck and dear, and all. Now
he told her that she had the best of it ; she having
a good life to stand by her, while his debaucheries
and ungodly life did always stare him in the face.
Now he told her the counsel that she often gave him
was good ; though he was so bad as not to take
it." [2]

But he recovered ; and, as his strength returned,
his good resolutions evaporated ; to the great distress
of his wife, who shortly after died of a broken
heart.

Mr. Badman, greatly to Attentive's surprise, was
not for marrying again in a hurry, and when asked
the reason would answer, " Who would keep a
cow of their own that can have a quart of milk for
a penny ? " However, he got drunk and was
entrapped into a promise by a woman in her own
ways as bad as he. They lived together for fourteen
or sixteen years until all their money was spent, and
then they parted.

But Mr. Badman's sins ultimately brought on him

[1] *Works*, iii, 645.   [2] *Ibid.*, p. 650.

the sinner's diseases, and he rapidly weakened with consumption; for all that he never showed any signs of penitence.

"Pray, how was he in his death?" asks Attentive; "was death strong upon him? or did he die with ease quietly?"

"As quiet as a lamb," answers Mr. Wiseman; but, as he takes care to point out, no judgment can be formed of a man's eternal state by his last moments, though to be sure with some men, such as commit suicide or die in despair, there is not much doubt; and he instances with full gory details the horrible end of John Cox of Northampton, who eviscerated himself with a razor.

After further talk on the end of the wicked, the sun grows low; Attentive takes his leave of Mr. Wiseman; and the book ends.

There must have been several very uncomfortable tradesmen in Bedford the day after the first copies of *Mr. Badman* were distributed, for a number of the examples are taken from Bunyan's own experiences. Individuals are not mentioned, as he carefully points out in his preface, lest he should lay them under disgrace and contempt; but in a small and tattling county town the anonymous sinner is soon fitted with a local habitation and a name. Moreover, it seems to be more than coincidence that a certain John Wileman (or Wildman) was giving much trouble to the congregation at this time.

At a Generall Church meeting at Cottenend the 2 day of November, 1680, John Wildman did at that Church meeting manage A charge against the congregation which he had drawne up, most of it in wrighting, and sent to us summe time before, in the manageing of which charge he was found extriordinary guilty of a kind of Railery and very great passion very much condemned by the whole congregation. Alsoe he was found guilty of slandering the congregation and brethren, in perticular our beloued and honnered brother Bunyan, in what he had spoken to Mr. Gibs. Alsoe he did desperately charge our brother and pastor: John Bunyan, with calling the sisters to know ther Husbands estates, in order to put a levy opon them wher In he was proued before the whole congregation an abominable lyer and slanderer of our beloved brother Bunyan ffor those causes with others the congregation did at that meeteing in Christ name with draw church comunyan from him with a joynt consent, not one so much as makeing the least sticke at it. And it was then Agreed opon that if the congregation did not perceaue repentance in him at the next church meeting he should be cast out of the Church.[1]

In his next book of importance, the *Holy War* (published in 1682), Bunyan returned to allegory, in the form of a chronicle history of the war between King Shaddai and Diabolus for the town of Mansoul, wherein is figured the original fall of man, his salvation through Christ, his falling away after conversion,

[1] *Church Book,* f. 68.

and his final restitution. As a story it is exciting reading.

King Shaddai had built the City of Mansoul for himself, but Diabolus, who was one of his revolted and banished servants, plotted revenge with his fellow-sufferers, as Satan in *Paradise Lost.* So they massed before the city, sat down before Ear-gate, and began to parley with the inhabitants. Captain Resistance having been killed by treachery, and Lord Innocent also, the inhabitants were easily persuaded to let Diabolus and his band march in. Thereupon Diabolus began to remodel the constitution, turning out the Lord Mayor and Mr. Recorder Conscience, putting in their places Lord Lustings and Mr. Forget-good, which proceedings were not unlike certain high-handed measures that had been taken in the town of Bedford about this time.[1]

When the King heard of the revolt, he began to take counsel with his son to recover Mansoul, which made Diabolus the more eager to corrupt the inhabitants, and this he did chiefly through the agency of Mr. Filth, who drew up an odious writing whereby he granted free licence to all his subjects to do whatever their lustful appetites prompted them to do. He also exhorted his subjects and armed them against the expected attack.

King Shaddai's first army was commanded by four generals, Captain Boanerges, Captain Conviction,

[1] Brown, p. 311.

Captain Judgment, and Captain Execution, who marched with flying colours up to the city, and a long parley followed. The captains tried to assault the town, but without success; so they sat down to besiege it. The town then opened another parley, and proposals were made for peace, on condition that the state of the town should remain as it was. A debate followed which ended in a riot in Mansoul, but still the besiegers were kept outside. The four captains therefore petitioned the King for reinforcements, and these were despatched under the King's own son, Prince Emmanuel.

Prince Emmanuel now began to make preparations for an assault, but first, like Tamburlane, he hung out a white flag to show that he offered mercy. Two days later he hung out the red flag which belonged to Captain Judgment; and at last a black flag to show defiance. But still the inhabitants refused to listen. So after very fierce fighting, the attack was pressed home and Prince Emmanuel entered the city.

There was now nothing left for the inhabitants but to submit, which after further parley they were obliged to do unconditionally and to send their prisoners to the Prince. But to their astonishment instead of putting them to death, he pardoned them, gave them new clothing, and sent them home with pipe and tabor.

The prisoners returned in triumph to the city to the intense joy of the inhabitants, who invited the

164

Prince to take up his residence with them. This he consented to do and entered the city with great triumphs, culminating in a grand banquet.

There remained, however, certain of the usurping Diabolonians to be dealt with. They were speedily put in prison and brought to trial, and, the jury having brought them in guilty, they were condemned and shortly afterwards executed, all but Mr. Incredulity, who had been one of Diabolus's Lord Mayors. He broke prison and rejoined his master outside.

Experience was now put in charge of the city and proceeded to remodel its constitution. For a time all went well, but before long Mr. Carnal-security began to stir up trouble, and the inhabitants of Mansoul grew less eager in their duties toward the Prince, who gradually withdrew from them, until they should acknowledge their offence. The Diabolonian lords that survived now saw their opportunity and were quickly intriguing with Diabolus, so that before long he appeared with a terrible army of Doubters and summoned the town to surrender. No answer being given, the assault was pressed home but repulsed valiantly. A little later the army of Mansoul determined on a sortie by night, but was repulsed and driven for refuge into the castle, leaving the town itself to the mercy of Diabolus, whose troops made great havoc of all that they could lay hands on.

Being in this state, the leaders in the castle drew

up a petition and sent to Prince Emmanuel, begging for his aid. Meanwhile Diabolus was about to try another plan of reducing Mansoul by withdrawing the army and introducing traders so that with returning prosperity the townsfolk should become negligent. But this scheme was frustrated by the appearance of Prince Emmanuel himself with his army.

The Diabolonians now led out their troops from the city to meet the relieving force, but they were thus caught between the Mansoul army and Prince Emmanuel, and annihilated, though the leaders escaped. So the Prince returned once more with triumph into his city.

Diabolus, however, was not yet finally defeated, and he drew together another army composed of Doubters and Bloodmen, and once more the town was invested, but the enemy were again defeated and many of them taken prisoner. Other Doubters, separated from their army, managed to find their way back into the city, notably old Mr. Evil-questioning. But they were soon arrested, brought up for trial and duly hanged. A warrant was then issued for Evil-questioning's children.

Finally, the town of Mansoul having been purged of its enemies, the Prince summoned the inhabitants into the market-place and there addressed them, ending with these words :

Remember therefore, O my Mansoul, that thou art beloved of me ; as I have therefore taught thee

to watch, to fight, to pray, and to make war against
my foes, so now I command thee to believe that my
love is constant to thee. O my Mansoul, how have
I set my heart, my love upon thee, watch. Behold,
I lay none other burden upon thee, than what thou
hast already, hold fast till I come.[1]

Such is a brief outline of *The Holy War*. It is a
most elaborate and ingenious allegory, and for that
very reason less successful as an appeal to conscience
than *The Pilgrim's Progress*, because the reader is
compelled all the time to admire the astonishing
ingenuity of the author. The idea of the human soul
as a community was not new ; it had been used
long ago in the fable of the belly and the members,
but there the symbolism was very simple. Used
on so vast a scale as in *The Holy War* it is less satisfactory because there is some confusion in the conception of Mansoul ; sometimes it stands for the
people, feeling fear, hope, or joy in the vicissitudes
of the campaign, at others for the town itself, wrecked
and rebuilt, static and material. The individual can
see his perplexities reflected in Christian's stumblings
he cannot so readily identify himself with the town
of Mansoul ; and in reading *The Holy War* he is
more interested in watching the progress of the
campaign than in considering its application to the
state of his own soul. But this is not to disparage

[1] *Works*, iii, 373.

Bunyan's skill; *The Holy War*, as a work of art, is the greatest English allegory.

A closer examination of *The Holy War* reveals some interesting traits in Bunyan's mentality. Both in *The Pilgrim's Progress* and *The Holy War* there are trial scenes which can be closely paralleled. In the *Progress* the good are tried by the wicked; the trial is a farce, the hearing of evidence and the verdict of the jury being but formal preliminaries to the passing of sentence. Critics have pointed out that Judge Jeffreys' methods on the bench were very similar. But the trials of the wicked in *The Holy War* are quite as arbitrary. Mr. Lustings, for instance, having stated his creed, the court answer, "There hath proceeded enough from his own mouth to lay him open to condemnation, wherefore set him by, jailer, and set Mr. Incredulity to the bar." It is curious that in the Prince Emmanuel's court the judge should follow the example of Caiaphas. In Mr. Incredulity's case, no witnesses are heard; he is condemned forthwith from his own words in answer to the indictment.

"So the town of Mansoul slew them according to the word of their Prince; but when the prisoners were brought to the cross to die, you can hardly believe what troublesome work Mansoul had of it to put the Diabolonians to death; for the men knowing that they must die, and every of them having implacable enmity in their heart to Mansoul, what did they but took courage at the cross, and there resisted the men of the town of Mansoul ? " [1]

Nothing showed up the wicked state of the condemned more clearly than this unruly behaviour at the scaffold.

Proceedings in Mansoul are sometimes even more summary. Lord Will-be-will, hearing of the pranks of Jolly and Grigish, the sons of Harmless-mirth, set spies on them, and then hanged them out of hand. This action is highly approved as a " Christian act." Another " brave act " was that of Captain Self-denial, who, finding that the townsfolk were inclined to favour Mr. Self-love, " took him from the crowd, and had him among the soldiers, and there he was brained."

There are some interesting details in the first triumphant entry of Prince Emmanuel, which suggest that Bunyan's sense of humour, though acute in small details, was not widely developed. The young men are ordered to ring the bells for joy; there was a time when Bunyan regarded bell-ringing and dancing as pastimes of the devil. Yet when the Prince enters in his royal chariot the elders of Mansoul dance before him. Then he entertains them at a feast " with all manners of outlandish food."

It was food that came from his Father's court, and so there was dish after dish set before them, and they

[1] *Works*, iii, 317.

were commanded freely to eat. But still when a fresh dish was set before them, they would whisperingly say to each other, " What is it ? " For they wist not what to call it. They drank also of the water that was made wine; and were very merry with him. There was music also all the while at the table, and man did eat angels' food, and had honey given him out of the rock. So Mansoul did eat the food that was peculiar to the court, yea, they had now thereof to the full [1]:

an admirable picture of the awe-struck countryman at his first state banquet.

But the restoration of Prince Emmanuel is very like the Restoration of King Charles the Second, and it is curious how closely the Puritan modelled the ceremonial of the King of the Heaven on the ceremonial of the English Court. That republicanism, which was an ideal in this world, had no place in the next; though indeed both in *The Holy War* and in *Paradise Lost* free speech and a limited form of democracy were allowed amongst the fallen angels. If the constitution and policy of Mansoul at times of prosperity is in any way a picture of the ideal puritan state, it explains and largely condones the Conventicle and Five Mile Acts; for the zealous Puritan was as hard-hearted as his opponent, but lacked the means to assert his will.

The second part of *The Pilgrim's Progress* was

[1] *Works*, iii, 308.

published in 1684, six years after the first, with which
it invites comparison. It is a more peaceful and
humane book, written in the evening of Bunyan's
life, and he looks at Christiana and her children with
the eyes of an elderly man, so that their pilgrimage
has that air of tranquillity which is so noticeable in
Shakespeare's *Tempest*. Christian had hewn his
way through the battle of life as a soldier; Christiana
visits his battlefields eight years afterwards, noticing
the war memorials and the old traces of struggle.
She loses her bottle where Christian had lost his
roll; but she has none of her husband's remorse,
and simply sends her little boy back to fetch it.
Though there are indeed difficulties and enemies,
none of them come very near to making Mr. Greatheart despair. He can even afford to be chivalrous
with Giant Maul.

When they had rested them, and taken breath,
they both fell to it again, and Mr. Greatheart with
a full blow, fetched the giant down to the ground.
" Nay, hold, and let me recover," quoth he; so Mr.
Greatheart fairly let him get up. So it to they went
again, and the giant missed but little of all-to-breaking
Mr. Greatheart's skull with his club.[1]

Greatheart indeed is of the Jack the Giant Killer
breed, and not a weak mortal soul.

As the second pilgrimage lacks the intensity of

[1] *Ibid.*, iii, 210.

the first, so is its religious message more sympathetic. Christian and Hopeful pushed through alone, leaving weaklings by the way; Mr. Greatheart adds the diffident believers to his little band, such as Mr. Feeble-mind and Mr. Ready-to-halt. Christian and Hopeful were caught by Giant Despair, and escaped from his castle with great difficulty; Greatheart leads the attack on Doubting Castle, slays the Giant, and rescues Mr. Despondency and his daughter Much-afraid, to conduct them with the others to the bank of the river.

As a work of art the first part is an allegory which appeals to the soul by its passion; the second is a novel with a religious purpose, written with greater art, but with less power, and its scenes and characters are even more alive and human. Mercy, for instance, is not mercy personified, but a real and very attractive young woman, and her wooing by Mr. Brisk is a piece of delightful humour.

Now, by that these Pilgrims had been at this place a week, Mercy had a visitor that pretended some goodwill unto her, and his name was Mr. Brisk, a man of some breeding, and that pretended to religion; but a man that stuck very close to the world. So he came once or twice, or more, to Mercy, and offered love unto her. Now Mercy was of a fair countenance, and therefore the more alluring.

Her mind also was, to be always busying of herself in doing; for when she had nothing to do for herself, she would be making of hose and garments for others, and would bestow them upon them that had need. And Mr. Brisk, not knowing where or how she disposed of what she made, seemed to be greatly taken, for that he found her never idle. " I will warrant her a good housewife," quoth he to himself.

Mercy then revealed the business to the maidens that were of the house, and inquired of them concerning him, for they did know him better than she. So they told her, that he was a very busy young man, and one that pretended to religion; but was, as they feared, a stranger to the power of that which was good.

" Nay then," said Mercy, " I will look no more on him : for I purpose never to have a clog to my soul."

Prudence then replied that there needed no great matter of discouragement to be given to him, her continuing so as she had begun to do for the poor, would quickly cool his courage.

So the next time he comes, he finds her at her old work, a-making of things for the poor. Then said he, " What! always at it ? " " Yes," said she, " either for myself or for others." " And what canst thou earn a day ? " quoth he. " I do these things," said she, " that I may be rich in good works, laying up in store a good foundation against the time to come, that I may lay hold on eternal life." " Why, prithee, what dost thou with them ? " said he. " Clothe the naked," said she. With that his countenance fell. So he forbore to come at her again, and when he was asked the reason why, he said, that Mercy was a pretty lass, but troubled with ill conditions.[1]

There is realism too in the description of Matthew's attack of the gripes and his mother's coaxing efforts to make him take his pill.

Some of the little sketches are very skilful, such as Madam Bubble : " Is she not a tall comely dame, something of a swarthy complexion ? Doth she not speak very smoothly, and give you a smile at the end of a sentence ? " Or again, Mrs. Lustings' party : " I was yesterday at Madam Wanton's, where we were as merry as the maids. For who do you think should be there, but I and Mrs. Love-the-flesh, and three or four more, with Mr. Lechery, Mrs. Filth, and some others. So there we had music, and dancing, and what else was meet to fill up the pleasure. And, I dare say, my lady herself is an admirably well-bred gentlewoman, and Mr. Lechery is as pretty a fellow." [2]

Or Valiant-for-truth (surely one of Cromwell's veterans) :

Then said Greatheart to Mr. Valiant-for-truth, " Thou hast worthily behaved thyself. Let me see thy sword." So he showed it him. When he had taken it in his hand, and looked thereon a while, he said, " Ha ! it is a right Jerusalem blade."

[1] *Works*, iii, 200.   [2] *Ibid.*, p. 177.

" It is so. Let a man have one of these blades, with a hand to wield it and skill to use it, and he may venture upon an angel with it. He need not fear its holding, if he can but tell how to lay on. Its edges will never blunt. It will cut flesh and bones, and soul and spirit, and all." [1]

It is Valiant-for-truth who sings the fine hymn—

> Who would true valour see,
>   Let him come hither ;
> One here will constant be,
>   Come wind, come weather.
>
> There's no discouragement
>   Shall make him once relent
> His first avow'd intent
>   To be a pilgrim.[2]

But nowhere is the contrast between the two parts more striking than in their endings. Christian and Hopeful cross the river and enter the city to a triumphant peal of trumpets and alleluiahs. Greatheart's band quietly wait on the bank, to cross over alone, one by one.

In process of time there came a post to the town again, and his business was with Mr. Ready-to-halt. So he inquired him out, and said to him, " I am come to thee in the name of him whom thou hast loved and followed, though upon crutches ; and my message is to tell thee, that he expects thee at his

[1] *Works*, iii., 233.   [2] *Ibid.*, p. 235.

table to sup with him, in his kingdom, the next day after Easter; wherefore prepare thyself for this journey."

Then he also gave him a token that he was a true messenger, saying, "I have broken thy golden bowl, and loosed thy silver cord."

After this, Mr. Ready-to-halt called for his fellow-pilgrims, and told them, saying, "I am sent for, and God shall surely visit you also." So he desired Mr. Valiant to make his will; and because he had nothing to bequeath to them that should survive him, but his crutches, and his good wishes, therefore thus he said, "These crutches I bequeath to my son that shall tread in my steps, with a hundred warm wishes that he may prove better than I have done."

Then he thanked Mr. Greatheart for his conduct and kindness, and so addressed himself to his journey. When he came at the brink of the river, he said, "Now I shall have no more need of these crutches, since yonder are chariots and horses for me to ride on." The last words he was heard to say was "Welcome life!" So he went his way.[1]

There is nothing in Bunyan so movingly beautiful as the gentle close of the second part of *The Pilgrim's Progress*.

At the end of the *Church Book* there is a page in Bunyan's handwriting headed "Of persons deceased in the congregation ffrom November 1681." Five names were entered together, covering the months

---

[1] *Works*, iii., 241.

of November and December, amongst them " our honoured Brother, Samuel ffenn, one of the Elders of this Congregation." Another batch of six who died between 30th August 1682 and 31st March 1683 was added later. It may be that in writing the last pages of *The Pilgrim's Progress* Bunyan had some of these names in mind.

In April 1683 John Wileman was again giving trouble ; a " frothy letter " was " presented to the congregation, wherein he counteth our dealing with him for his correction and amendment scuffling and fooling, and so desires a corispondance."

The answer sent to him, if firm, was mild. The entry is in Bunyan's handwriting.

ffriend Wileman,
Your letter has bin plainly read before us, and since you have bin withdrawn ffrom by the church ffor lying, railing, and scandalizing of the church in generall, and som of the brethren in perticuler : It is expected

1. That there be the signes of true repentance found in you for the same

2. And also that you bring from the hands of those in the countrey before whom you have abused us som signe of their satisfaction concerning your repentance before we can admitt you againe into our commuion.

Written for you and sent you by order of the congregation.[1]

The letter was attested by Bunyan signing first, and fifteen other witnesses.

After the death of Charles the Second, Bunyan was able to preach more openly.

When Mr. Bunyan preached in London, if there were but one day's notice given, there would be more people come together to hear him preach than the meeting-house would hold. I have seen to hear him preach, by my computation, about twelve hundred at a morning lecture, by seven o'clock, on a working day, in the dark winter time. I also computed about three thousand that came to hear him one Lord's-day, at London, at a town's end meeting-house ; so that half were fain to go back again for want of room, and then himself was fain, at a back door, to be pulled almost over people to get upstairs to his pulpit.[1]

Meanwhile he was still writing, and between 1684 and 1688 he printed *A Holy Life the Beauty of Christianity*, *A Caution to Stir up to Watch against Sin*, *A Discourse upon the Pharisee and the Publican*, and a book of rhymes for children.

In 1688 was published one of the best of his sermons, *The Jerusalem Sinner saved, or good news for the vilest of men*, intended to persuade the worst sinner that there was room for him within God's mercy. " I have been vile myself, but have obtained

[1] Doe, printed in *Works*, iii, 766.

mercy," Bunyan says in his preface ; " and I would have my companions in sin partake of mercy too : and therefore I have writ this little book." Jerusalem was the worst of cities, yet with Jerusalem were the Apostles ordered to begin their mission ; and the first Church was made up of Jerusalem sinners. How then can a sinner doubt or fear the damnation of his soul, if he be penitent, however bad a life he had led, or however many sins he had committed ? Bunyan speaks by experience ; he was one of the great sin-breeders, like a verminous man ; wherefore Christ took him first. Nothing, except the sin against the Holy Ghost, can prevent a man coming to Christ. " But," answers the doubter, " I am a reprobate." And the answer is,

Now thou talkest like a fool, and meddlest with what thou understandest not : no sin, but the sin of final impenitence, can prove a man a reprobate ; and I am sure thou hast not arrived as yet unto that ; therefore thou understandest not what thou sayest, and makest groundless conclusions against myself. Say thou art a sinner, and I will hold with thee ; say thou art a great sinner, and I will say so too ; yea, say thou art one of the biggest sinners, and spare not ; for the text yet is beyond thee, is yet betwixt hell and thee ; " Begin at Jerusalem " has yet a smile upon thee ; and thou talkest as if thou wast a reprobate, and that the greatness of thy sins do prove thee so to be, when yet they of Jerusalem were not such, whose sins, I dare say, were such, both for bigness

and heinousness, as thou art not capable of committing beyond them; unless now, after thou
hast received conviction that the Lord Jesus is the
only Saviour of the world, thou shouldest wickedly
and despitefully turn thyself from him, and conclude
he is not to be trusted to for life, and so crucify him
for a cheat afresh.[1]

Even if God is silent to the sinner, it is no ground
of despair, so long as there is a promise in the Bible
that God will in no wise cast away the coming sinner,
and so long as he invites the Jerusalem sinner to come
unto him.

For all that, Bunyan did not abandon the doctrine
of election. On 19th August 1688 he preached his
last sermon, on John i. 33, and the message is the
old one, though a little modified. There is in man
a will to be vile and a will to be saved; but natural
desires after the things of another world are no
argument to prove a man will go to heaven.

I am not a free-willer, I do abhor it; yet there is not
the wickedest man but he desires, some time or other,
to be saved; he will read some time or other, or,
it may be, pray, but this will not do: " It is not of
him that willeth, nor of him that runneth, but of
God that sheweth mercy." There is willing and
running, and yet to no purpose (Rom. ix. 16). Israel,
which followed after the law of righteousness, have

---

[1] *Works*, i, 88.

not obtained it (ver. 30). Here, I do not understand, as if the apostle had denied a virtuous course
of life to be the way to heaven ; but that a man
without grace, though he have natural gifts, yet
he shall not obtain privilege to go to heaven, and
be the son of God. Though a man without grace
may have a will to be saved, yet he cannot have that
will God's way.[1]

Three days after this sermon was preached a
young man, a neighbour of his, appealed to Bunyan.
He had fallen out with his father, who was proposing
to disinherit him ; he therefore begged Bunyan
to intercede for him and prepare the way for a re-
conciliation. Bunyan consented, rode out to Reading
and mollified the father ; but on the way back he
was caught in a violent storm of rain and returned
to his lodgings wet through. A violent attack of
fever followed, and on the 31st of August he died.
He was buried in Bunhill Fields.

Bunyan's character at the end of his life is thus
described by one who knew him :

He appeared in countenance to be a stern and rough
temper ; but in his conversation mild and affable, not
given to loquacity or much discourse in company,
unless some urgent occasion required it ; observing
never to boast of himself, or his parts, but rather
seem low in his own eyes, and submit himself to the

---

[1] *Works*, ii, 756.

judgment of others ; abhorring lying and swearing,
being just in all that lay in his power to his word,
not seeming to revenge injuries, loving to reconcile
differences, and make friendship with all ; he had
a sharp quick eye, accomplished with an excellent
discerning of persons, being of good judgment and
quick wit. As for his person, he was tall of stature,
strong-boned, though not corpulent, somewhat of
a ruddy face, with sparkling eyes, wearing his hair
on his upper lip, after the old British fashion ; his
hair reddish, but in his later days, time had sprinkled
it with grey ; his nose well set, but not declining
or bending, and his mouth moderate large ; his
forehead somewhat high, and his habit always plain
and modest. [1]

The news of Bunyan's death soon reached Bedford,
and the sense of utter loss felt by his congregation
is shown in the entries in the *Church Book* :

Wednesday the 4th of September was kept in
prayer And Humilyation for this Heavy Stroak upon
us yᵉ Death of dare Bro: Bunyan

Apoynted allso that wednsday next be kept in
praire and Humiliation on the same account. . . .

Tusday yᵉ 18 of Septʳ was yᵉ wholl congregation
mett to Humble themselves before god by ffasting
& Prayer for his Hevy & sevear stroak upon us
takeing away our Honoured Bro: Bunyan by death.[2]

To his own people Bunyan was most famous as

[1] *Works*, i, 64.   [2] *Church Book*, f. 73.

a preacher, but it is as a writer that his name survives. With many great authors the work is so much greater than the man that there is often a desire to escape from the facts of his biography, due to something more than mere impatience with scholarly pedantry. With Bunyan this is not so; the man was as great as his work. He had many limitations; no English writer of the first rank began with more disadvantages; he lacked education and wide reading; he never mixed with other men of letters; he was nurtured on a theological diet of much locust and little wild honey.

But he had certain advantages which more than compensated. What he had missed in his education he gained by a very wide observation of men in every variety of emotional experience, and he had the acutest perception, ever noting, comparing, understanding the workings of the human mind. He had an immense courage, a quality not always conspicuous in the artistic temperament; courage indeed of this kind is so rare that the man who can endure finds his reward in this world, as Bunyan was rewarded by the religious devotion of his many followers.

Then there was, after his conversion, a certainty in his creed which sustained him and drove him on, so that when lesser men would doubt, waver or compromise, Bunyan at the height of persecution or misunderstanding only became firmer and sterner.

183

Yet this hardness was his only refuge from despair; it is not natural for a man of such sympathy and understanding to be hard-hearted, and in favourable times his true nature shows itself in such works as *The Strait Gate*, the second part of *The Pilgrim's Progress*, *Come and Welcome*, and that last pastoral office at Reading. This, rather than the author of *Instructions for the Ignorant*, was the real Bunyan.

Most of all Bunyan had something to say, not indeed always—few writers have repeated themselves so often—but at times overpoweringly, and his whole life from the time of his first marriage onwards was spent in learning and practising the difficult art of speaking, not only at a weekly meeting for the edification of a complacent congregation, but to convert the sinner and to strengthen him under persecution. He had too the advantage of a keenly critical congregation, as learned in the Scriptures as he, and ready enough to appreciate an argument, to find flaws in unsound doctrine, or to respond to a moving appeal. There were ten years of this training behind him when he wrote *Grace Abounding*, more than twenty before he began *The Pilgrim's Progress*.

Few even amongst professed ministers of the gospel now believe in Bunyan's conception of the universe, and his immediate message has lost its meaning in the modern world. Many of his books survive as little more than curious examples of an extinct theology. But four stand out—*Grace Abounding*, *The Pilgrim's Progress*, *Mr. Badman*, and *The Holy War*—perennial monuments of a man who was greater than his creed. These are alive with the abiding spirit of man.

INDEX

INDEX

Abiss, Sister, 118
Act for restoring ejected ministers, 69
Arthur, Thomas, 108, 109

Badman, The Life and Death of Mr., 135, 152–61
Baldock Fair, 121
Baptism, 115
Bardolf, John, 107
Barkwood, Lord, 76
Battison, Thomas, 107
Beaumont, Agnes, 118–22
Bedford, 31, 117, 118, 144, 163, 182
Bedford, Congregational Church at, 34; original founders, 34; principles of foundation, 34; acts and troubles of, 101–11
Bedford, St. John's Church, 53
Bedford, the poor women of, 27, 28, 29, 144
Bentley, Margaret, 14
Blake, William, 40
Bosworth, Sister, 34
Breeden, Brother, 103
Brown, Dr. John, 125
Browne, Sir Thomas, 54
Bunyan, Elizabeth (second wife), 63, 76
Bunyan John, baptized, 14; unhappy childhood, 16–17; youth, 17; military service, 18; first marriage, 21; leanings to religion, 22; ceases bell-ringing and dancing, 25; sensitiveness to rhythms, 27; habit of dramatising experience, 27; outward reformation, 24–30; dream of poor women, 28; encounter with a Ranter, 31; intense mental conflict, 30–47; meets Gifford,

33; controversy with Quakers, 39; joins Bedford community, 47, 53; conviction of grace, 47–9; removes to Bedford, 53; *Some Gospel Truths opened* and its *Vindication*, 53; proposed as deacon, 54; *A Few Sighs from Hell*, 55; first wife dies, 63; marries second wife, 63; *Doctrine of the Law and Grace Unfolded*, 63–8; arrest, 69; trial, 71; attempts at release, 77–8; imprisonment, 77–8; *Christian Behaviour*, 82–9; *One Thing is Needful*, 89–91; *The Holy City*, 91–4; *Grace Abounding*, 94–7; second imprisonment, 101; takes active part in church affairs, 101–11; *Confession of Faith*, 112; infant son baptized, 115; elected pastor, 115; case of Agnes Beaumont, 118; *Reprobation Asserted*, 122; *Light for them that sit in Darkness*, 126; *Christian Behaviour*, 129; third imprisonment, begins *Pilgrim's Progress*, 141; *Mr. Badman*, 152; *The Holy War*, 162; *Second Part of Pilgrim's Progress*, 170; *Jerusalem Sinner Saved*, 178–80; last sermon, 180; death, 181; character, 181
Bunyan, Mary, 63
Bunyan Thomas, senior, 14
Bunyan, Thomas, junior, 14
Burton, John, 53, 62

Caiaphas, 168
Caution to stir up Watch against Sin, 178
Chamberlain, Sister, 54
Characters, Books of, 136

189

INDEX

INDEX